FRIENDS
AT THE
TABLE

FRIENDS

AT THE

TABLE

The Ultimate
Supper Club Cookbook

DEBI SHAWCROSS

FRANKLIN GREEN
PUBLISHING
www.franklingreenpublishing.com

Published by Franklin Green Publishing
P. O. Box 2828
Brentwood, TN 37024
www.franklingreenpublishing.com

Photographs by Ron Manville
Page design by Mandi Cofer
Food Styling by Cathy Hinton
Salon Services provided by Mango Salon

EAN: 978-1-93648-700-4

Printed in China
10 9 8 7 6 5 4 3 2 1

For **Jeff**, **Emma** and **Jane**

You provide love, happiness and joy in my life.

CONTENTS

WHAT IS A SUPPER CLUB?

A Nostalgic Glance at Years Gone By

A supper club in the 1930s and 40s was a gathering place for people to meet and enjoy an evening of fine dining, drinks, and usually live musical entertainment. The setting was semi-formal, which may have required a tie. The menu often included "surf and turf," mashed potatoes, and Yorkshire pudding. These supper clubs launched many musical careers and introduced the "doggie bag." Tommy Dorsey, Jimmy Dorsey, Gene Krupa, Glenn Miller, and Benny Goodman are some of the well-known musicians who performed in supper clubs around the country during the swing/big band era. Picture Desi Arnaz at a club playing to an audience of stylishly dressed patrons seated in club–chair style booths and sipping martinis.

The nostalgic appeal of these early supper clubs is attributed, at least in part, to the longing to recapture a period when people made time for each other. In today's world where we eat many meals on the run, an intimate dinner with friends is a great luxury.

The Modern Version and Its Possibilities

We propose taking the elements of supper clubs gone by and transforming them into an evening at home—a time and place where you get together with friends in a festive atmosphere and celebrate a mutual passion for fine food. Most importantly, these evenings will facilitate a deeper connection with people you care about.

Your modern-day supper club will meet regularly, on a schedule the members choose. Another point to consider is the pooling of your culinary resources to create a four-course meal without anyone spending all day in the kitchen. Your club could include a gourmet meal where each course is assigned to different members to be prepared at home and brought to the host's home for serving—in other words, job sharing to create the ultimate dinner party.

Your iPod's favorite playlists could replace the live musical entertainment heard in the supper clubs of the 1930s and '40s, setting an ambiance of cool comfort.

You will have the opportunity to try your hand at "tablescapes," using candles and fresh flowers. And you will be able to enjoy an evening of fine dining without the expense of a restaurant bill! We know all of these things from experience.

But perhaps the hardest thing about getting your supper club up and running is deciding what to make. You may identify a wonderful entrée, but aren't sure what flavors to capture and pair with it. That's where I come in. I've written this book so that you may take one of my menus and bring it to life adding your own personal touches. I've included menus that are grand and elegant, some more casual and ethnic, and others that are a mix of it all.

Forming Your Club—a Culinary Adventure

Cooking and food have never been more popular, a fact supported by the introduction of the Food Network in 1993, which has grown by leaps and bounds ever since. Morning news programs have also brought cooking before our eyes, adding live cooking segments to their daily shows. In addition to the popularity of cooking shows on television, there is a plethora of magazines to choose from that cater to every aspect of culinary interest. Have you found yourself ooing and ahing while watching dishes prepared on the screen or in print? You probably have found yourself wanting to try the recipes at home with friends and family. Food begins as a visual experience. If you like what you see, your sense of smell draws the flavors onto your taste buds, where you complete the journey. Why not couple your love of food and cooking with an evening at home spent with friends? Sounds like a dinner party, right? A supper club is a dinner party of sorts; only a supper club is not just about the food. Members of a supper club commit to meet regularly with common goals in mind. This built-in element of continuity enables the supper club to grow and strengthen relationships. A supper club is designed to build relationships on a deep, ongoing level.

While writing this book, I talked with several people who participate in supper clubs. All agreed that they found their supper clubs very fulfilling.

Tom and Tracey formed their supper club with some of their neighbors at a time in their lives when they all had very young children. They had taken a break from entertaining during the sleep-deprived diaper-changing years, and were ready to enjoy some uninterrupted conversation and adult time. They are forming close friendships as they watch their children grow, as well as developing their culinary skills.

In Garret and Molly's supper club, the couples share the cooking responsibilities. They enjoy the time they spend in the kitchen together talking and laughing as they cook.

Jack and Bettie have been in a supper club for more than forty years! In their supper club the husbands do all of the cooking and all of the clean up. In their generation, the wives handled most of the day-to-day cooking, so this offered an opportunity for a little role reversal, not to mention a little break for the wives!

Sound inviting? Let me help you get started on your culinary adventure.

Organizing Your Culinary Capers

Defining Your Group

A supper club begins by defining your group. Ideally a supper club involves eight to ten people. You are creating an intimate dining experience, where everyone can sit comfortably at the table and conversation invites itself.

Who will be your members? Are you a group of young married couples eager to entertain? A group of friends looking for a means to strengthen friendships? Are you interested in meeting other couples in your neighborhood? (This is very popular in retirement communities.) Or are you a group of professional single peoples interested in networking and expanding relationships? Are you new to the area and wanting to form friendships? Perhaps you are a combination of some of these groups.

You may wish to include the same core group of people at each gathering, or you may wish to set a core group of people with an additional two guests who rotate in each gathering at the host's invitation, to create a slightly new mix of people each time. There is not an "official rule book" or anyone who will be checking up on you, so have fun with the options!

Most importantly, to reap the benefits of a successful supper club you must agree on a common goal. Are you all intent on trying out your best culinary skills? Or are you more interested in the socializing aspect? Sharing a similar level of cooking experience can make for a more cohesive group. If you are all budding cooks, you can learn together. Similarly, if you are superb chefs, you can appreciate each other's talents. A mix of skill levels works just fine too, as long as everyone understands and agrees on their expectations. This is a club and every club needs some ground rules.

Getting Organized

Now that you have defined your supper club group, it's time to get organized. Set an informal meeting (perhaps at a local coffee shop), where you can discuss and agree upon how your supper club will work.

Decide how often you would like to meet. Do you want to meet every month? Every other month? Maybe quarterly works best for everyone's schedules. In order for your supper club to operate smoothly, you need to commit to a schedule and stick with it.

This is a good time to discuss things like food allergies, aversions, or preferences. Are there any vegetarians in the group? It's much better to have an understanding up front of what types of foods people are most interested in eating or experimenting with. The supper club experience will hopefully expand your culinary palates; just make sure you are all in agreement. That accomplished, decide who will host the first gathering.

Sharing the Adventure

The next thing to decide is how the menu preparation will be handled. One approach is for the host(s) to select two menus and take a vote. Or the host could decide on the menu without a vote. In either case, recipes for all courses could be distributed. For your supper club, you may want the host to choose the entrée and all other members select a recipe to complement the entrée. These dishes would be prepared at members' homes and then brought to the host's home to complete the meal. For example, Fred and Ginger bring the appetizer, Bob and Helen bring the salad, and Sabrina and Alan bring the dessert. Visit my Web site (www.debishawcross.com) for additional menu and party ideas.

Note: When bringing a course to the host's home for service, it should require very little preparation after you arrive. Bring a salad in a serving bowl with the dressing ready to add and toss. With an appetizer that needs heating, bring it on a baking sheet or in a container ready to pop in the oven. Making the host's job as easy as possible should be everyone's goal.

If your group is a bit more adventurous in the kitchen, the host may want to prepare the entire menu from appetizer though dessert. This option is a lot more work for the host, but offers a "free night" for the other guests. And the next time the group gathers at the table, the host will be a guest and have the night off.

At this point you know who your supper club members are, how often you will meet, and how you will handle menu preparation. Now for the next step in planning. Will you be serving cocktails or wine with your meal? If so, who will provide them? Here are some options:

- *The host provides the entrée, beverages, cocktails, and wine for the meal.*

- *Each member brings a course to the host's home with a bottle of wine that they've paired with it. You may wish to pair champagne with the appetizer, Pinot Grigio with the soup, and Pinot Noir with the appetizer.*

- *One member (or couple) of your supper club selects wine to be paired with each course and shares the qualities/characteristics of each with the group. Your local wine shop can be a terrific resource. This could be a fun way to expand your knowledge of wine. You may want to keep a record of the wines you especially enjoyed. What elements in the wine sparked interest in the food? Why? This would be a great tool in future meal planning.*

- *You could hire a professional sommelier for the evening. This is becoming popular in many larger cities where sommeliers are moving outside of restaurants to do in-home wine education evenings. In this case, the group would provide the menu to the sommelier, who would in turn pair wine (defined within your budget) to accompany your meal. The sommelier would also educate your group on the wine selected. The fee for a professional sommelier runs from $200 to $300 per hour and is typically a two-hour event. Your supper club could split the fee among the members.*

Budget

Budget may or may not be an issue for your supper club. Simply rotating the host's role and course assignment may be the best way to handle the cost of ingredients. (Everyone pays for the course they are preparing.) You may wish to follow this structure but divvy up the costs of the wine and cocktails among everyone. Or you may wish to keep a log of all expenses for each gathering and divide the cost equally. Decide what will work best for all of you. This is a group activity, so everyone's preferences should be addressed. And remember, if something is not working, it can be changed at any time with the group's consensus.

Style of Serving

How will the food be served? Do you prefer to serve restaurant style, where individual plates are prepared and carried to the table? Or is your preference family style, where all of the food is brought to the table in serving dishes and passed from friend to friend? If serving restaurant style, recruit a few people from your group to help serve. (The host should not be scrambling to get things on the table. We want this to be relaxed and fun.)

Cleanup

The not-so-fun part. Cleanup can be the host's job after everyone leaves, or you may wish to all pitch in and get it done. It's up to you. One person I interviewed about their supper club has children. They hire a baby-sitter to stay upstairs with the children, while their evening event takes place downstairs. After the children are asleep, they pay the sitter an additional sum to help with the dishes.

Thinking Ahead

Now that we've talked about getting your supper club organized and running, let's talk about how you will continue moving forward.

During your first dinner gathering, decide who your next host will be and set the next date. This is the best time to put your date on your calendar and commit. Next, determine your menu and assign the courses to your members. Be sure to rotate the course assignment so that each person gets the chance to make dessert. (Proceed according to the plan you chose, or move to another plan if the evening's experience suggests change may be in order.) You want to keep things interesting.

One way to add interest to your supper club is to vary the theme of your evenings. Following are a few ideas:

- *Vary the dress code for you, your table, and your menu. Choose some nights to dress for a formal evening–with your best dishes and an elegant menu. Keep some nights casual with your favorite comfortable jeans and a bowl of chips and salsa. Allow for evenings with everything in between.*

- *Plan an ethnic night. Decorate your table and play music that fits the theme. (Visit my Web site ,www.debishawcross.com, for some fun ideas.)*

- *Have a masquerade party.*

- *Pick up a version of Table Topics. These games offer wonderful ideas using conversation-starting cards.*

- *Plan a supper club "field trip" and travel to a weekend retreat.*

- *Take a hike (or) attend a concert and enjoy a picnic dinner during or afterward.*

Other things to consider once your supper club is up and running:

Do you want to change anything about your supper club? If so, talk to each other about it. It's important to keep communication lines open. If there are things you really enjoy about your supper club, talk about that as well.

You may want to take photos at each supper club gathering to capture the memories. Keeping a journal of the triumphs and failures can also be fun. Not all dishes will be four-star, and that's okay. The goal of a supper club is to work together, building relationships based on common experiences.

Planning for the Adventure

In the cooking classes I teach, my students are always interested in finding recipes that can be prepared ahead of time. To some the idea of entertaining seems much too great a project to take on. I hear stories in class of people frantically peeling potatoes moments before guests ring the doorbell. When the guests do arrive, they are too exhausted to enjoy themselves because they have spent the whole day in the kitchen working at warp speed. That is just not fun, and frankly if that is how it had to be, I don't think I would ever entertain either! When your guests arrive, you should feel calm and the energy in your house should reflect that spirit. You should have everything ready, with few things left to handle. Imagine the following scenario: when your doorbell rings, music is playing in the background, setting the tone for the evening;

candles are flickering, adding to the ambiance; and you answer the door, relaxed and ready to have fun.

You are probably asking how you are supposed to do that. It's true, it is not going to happen on its own. You will be doing some work—however, you will not be doing everything in one day! As a cooking class instructor, I have to be organized. I often have eighteen people attending my class, four nights in a row, who are counting on me to demonstrate each course of the menu in a timely manner and to present them with a delicious meal they can sit down and enjoy.

How do I tackle such a feat? I treat each menu as a project. I begin with a strategy. I break down each menu and plan out how far in advance I can make each item. If there is an opportunity to make something and freeze it, I definitely seize that opportunity. Next I put together a timeline and a schedule that leads me right up to the hour before guests arrive. This last hour is reserved to put the final touches on things and relax. When my doorbell rings, I feel confident and ready to have a great time with my friends.

I've taken my cooking class "game plan" and applied it to the menus in this book. You will find a Plan Ahead countdown schedule for each menu. There are some elements in planning your dinner that are universal.

Planning Your Menu

The first thing you need to do is decide on a menu. If you are hosting the supper club in your home, you will have a few extra details to attend to. If you will be dividing up the courses, however, you won't be spending nearly as much time in the kitchen. If you are preparing the entire menu, you will be able to use my Plan Ahead guide to accomplish it all.

Planning Your Table

As a host or hostess, you need to think about what you want your table to look like. Consider the menu—is it regional? Incorporate elements that include the season. The menu sets the tone for the table and the music. This is the time to make sure you have everything you need to create the perfect atmosphere to complement your meal. This part of the planning can start up to a month ahead of time. Make certain to check your tablecloth. You do not want to wait until the day of your gathering to realize the tablecloth you thought was just right is too small or has a huge stain on it! Tip: Layering different textures and fabrics can add character to your table.

What kind of candles will you use? Grouping them in different sizes and heights adds interest. Floating candles are a romantic way to dress the table. Will you add flowers to the table in one vase or several smaller ones? Take a look in your backyard—greens clipped from your hedges can add a nice feel to the table when mixed with flowers and candles.

Dishes? You can't go wrong with white. Food leaps off the plate from a white background. You can add color with garnishes and sauces. Or you can mix colors and patterns in your plates to add visual interest. Layering a white dinner plate with a colored salad plate and patterned dessert plate can be really fun. I like to use different place settings around the table. Sometimes it's difficult to decide or commit to one pattern. And you know what? You can be as creative as you want.

You do not need fancy china and crystal to entertain. You can dress up any table with the addition of a few fun accessories. I've found some great tea-light holders, plates, chargers, and other goodies at my local dollar store and flea markets. And your friends and family can be a great resource. They might have the perfect platter, candleholders, or flatware for your table. You can begin decorating your table five or so days before your supper club meets. (If you use your table daily, at least gather the elements together.) Take care of these details before you begin doing the food preparation that will take place closer to the event. Tip: Flowers can be arranged in vases a day ahead.

Planning for Equipment

Now that you have the table squared away, think about what you may need to prepare your meal. Do you have all of the necessary equipment? Do you have the right-sized sauté pan? If you are doing pan-seared scallops, will you need to sear in batches, or do you need a larger pan? Do you need to purchase ramekins or a torch for the crème brûlée you are making?

Planning for Wine and Music

Once you have done your initial planning, it's time to make a trip to the store for candles and other needed items. Take this opportunity to purchase the wine you will be pairing with your meal. Will you be serving wine before dinner? Buy this well ahead of time.

Music plays an important part in setting the mood for your evening. From the moment your guests arrive, they should be greeted with your selection. Be prepared ahead of time. Load up your iPod with tunes for the beginning of the evening (music to greet your guests), dinner music to enjoy with your meal, and music to end your evening. This can be done at least a month ahead of time.

Grocery Shopping

Take a look at your shopping list. (For each menu in this book, I have provided a Shopping List for you.) Divide the list into items that can be purchased one week ahead, two days ahead, down to things that can't be purchased until the day of (like seafood).

Cleaning

Clean your house a few days ahead of time, so that you just have touch-up to do on the day of your event. If you have silver to polish, take care of it well in advance. The day of your supper club gathering, run your dishwasher and put the dishes away by late afternoon, so that you have an empty dishwasher ready to load.

Food Prep and Cooking

Everyone wants to have most or all of the cooking done before their guests arrive so that they are free to visit. One of the first things people in my cooking classes ask is "Can this be made ahead of time? If so, how far in advance?"

Strategize. Treat this like a project with tasks. I break down each menu item and plan out how far in advance I can make it and when possible, freeze ahead. Then I put together a timeline and schedule to follow.

Before doing any cooking, have everything washed, prepped, and chopped. Place all of your ingredients in little bowls ready to be accessed when needed in your recipe. There is a French cooking term for this—*Mise en Place*—meaning "everything in its place." Even when cooking for my family of four I follow this rule. If a recipe calls for a quick sauté of garlic, followed by deglazing the pan with chicken broth, you do not want to be fumbling with a can opener and chicken broth as the garlic scorches, left unattended. Have everything ready and waiting to go.

Well-Stocked Pantry

In line with having things ready to go, here's a list of things I keep stocked in my pantry:

Extra-virgin olive oil	Vegetable broth	Sliced almonds
Peanut oil	Chicken broth	Pine nuts
Canola oil	Beef broth	Pecans
Sesame oil	Worcestershire sauce	Walnuts
Red wine vinegar	Arborio rice	Garlic
Balsamic vinegar	Brown rice	Red wine
White wine vinegar	Jasmine rice	White wine
Rice vinegar	Bulgur wheat	Coconut milk
Apple cider vinegar	Couscous	Chile-garlic sauce
Tomato paste	Panko bread crumbs	Fish sauce
Sun-dried tomatoes	Cornmeal	Oyster sauce
Canned plum tomatoes	Kosher salt	Shallots
Capers	Sea salt	Onions
Canned chipotle chiles in adobo sauce	Black peppercorns	Hoisin sauce
	Instant espresso powder	

I have a huge selection of spices, and always make sure I have:

Chipotle chile powder	Coriander
New Mexico chile powder	Dry mustard
Ancho chile powder	Curry powder
Cumin	

In my fridge, I always have a few key items to accessorize a salad or garnish a dish:

Parmigiano-Reggiano	Feta cheese
Blue cheese	Cilantro
Goat cheese	

Get Ready, Get Set, Go!

If you are new at cooking, and want to boost your confidence, do a trial run of your dish or menu. Your family and neighbors will love it! If you practice, you will learn. Knowledge and experience provide confidence. Being prepared takes away stress. You now have the information you need so that when your doorbell rings, you will be ready to greet your guests with a smile and have fun. So go ahead and turn the page. Pick out a menu and begin planning your supper club dinner.

I hope these recipes help you create lasting memories with your friends at the table through-out the years to come.

–Cheers!

FALL FAVORITES

Fall is one of my favorite times of year. The harvest is coming to an end, the leaves begin to change, and the air gets chilly. Fall takes me back to my childhood with memories of picking apples, eating warm cinnamon-sugar doughnuts, and drinking crisp apple cider—traditions I now share with my children.

As the days grow shorter, I crave heartier ingredients and full-flavored foods. I enjoy nothing more than coming inside and getting cozy by a fire for an evening with family and friends.

Shopping List

Produce

- 1 large shallot
- 1 bunch tarragon
- 1 lemon
- 4 Belgian endive spears
- 1 bunch Italian parsley
- 3 large onions
- 4 pounds butternut squash
- 1 bunch chives
- 1 garlic bulb
- 1 bunch rosemary
- 1 bunch fresh thyme
- 1 large fennel bulb
- 6 large apples

Note: My favorite apple for pies is Jonagold—not too sweet, not too tart, and they hold their shape. I really like to go with apples that are local to your area. Rome and Macoun apples are also good choices.

Meat and dairy

- 1 (4-pound) boneless center cut pork roast
- 8 ounces pancetta
- 3 ounces Roquefort cheese
- 6 ounces goat cheese
- 3 ounces Stilton cheese
- ½ cup Parmigiano-Reggiano cheese
- 1 pound unsalted butter
- 2 eggs

Frozen foods

- 3 (10-ounce) packages frozen spinach

Other groceries

- Extra-virgin olive oil
- White wine vinegar
- ⅓ cup walnuts
- Dried sage
- Cayenne pepper
- Ground cinnamon
- Ground ginger
- Ground nutmeg
- Brown sugar
- Salt
- Pepper
- All-purpose flour
- Sugar
- 4 quarts chicken broth
- ½ cup oil-packed sun-dried tomatoes
- 1 cup panko bread crumbs
- 1 roll butcher's cotton twine
- Aluminum foil
- Plastic wrap

Wine and spirits

- 4 cups red wine
- 2 cups port wine

Plan Ahead

1 day ahead:
Make soup
Make port wine sauce

8 hours ahead:
Make filling for endive cups
Prepare pork through step just before searing

6 hours ahead:
Bake pie

4 hours ahead:
Make spinach cakes

3 hours ahead:
Remove pork roulade from refrigerator and prepare to put into oven

2 hours ahead:
Fill endive cups

Endive Cups Filled with Roquefort, Lemon, and Walnuts

Roasted Butternut Squash Soup

Pork Roulade with Pancetta, Fennel, and Port Wine Sauce

Spinach Cakes

Apple Crumble Pie

The Roquefort in the endive cups will get your taste buds flying. I love the way the flavors of sweet and salty play together in these dishes. The amazing aroma drifting through your house as the roulade roasts in your oven will have your guests saying "yummm" as soon as they walk in the door.

WINE PAIRING: Start with a Riesling and move to a Merlot.

EQUIPMENT: food processor, butcher's twine

Tip: Many herbs such as rosemary, oregano, thyme, and chives are perennial and can endure the winter months in most areas of the country. If you have a little sunny place in your yard, try planting an herb garden; herbs are pretty self-sufficient. I am not much of a gardener, but sure do enjoy going out into my yard to clip what I need for a recipe. If you are purchasing herbs at the market and only use a small amount from your bunch, look for ways to incorporate them into other ingredients you may already have in your kitchen: blend chopped herbs into mayonnaise to jazz up a sandwich; add herbs to olive oil to make your own infused oil; and extra herbs always make a terrific garnish.

ENDIVE CUPS FILLED WITH
ROQUEFORT, LEMON, AND WALNUTS

1 large shallot, minced
1 tablespoon chopped fresh tarragon
½ cup extra-virgin olive oil
2 tablespoons white wine vinegar
¾ cup (about 3 ounces) Stilton cheese, crumbled
⅓ cup toasted walnuts, chopped
1 teaspoon lemon zest
    Salt and freshly ground pepper
4 Belgian endive spears, separated into spears
¼ cup chopped fresh Italian parsley

Combine shallots and tarragon in a medium bowl. Meanwhile, place the oil and vinegar in a small saucepan. Bring mixture to a slow simmer, swirling the pan occasionally. Stir in the Stilton and pour over salad mixture. Toss to coat. Stir in the toasted walnuts and lemon zest. Season with salt and freshly ground pepper. Cover; chill at least 30 minutes or up to 8 hours. Fill the endive spears with 2 teaspoons of salad. Sprinkle with chopped fresh Italian parsley to garnish.

8 servings

ROASTED BUTTERNUT SQUASH SOUP

½ cup unsalted butter
2 large onions, chopped
4 pounds butternut squash, peeled, cubed
1 tablespoon dried rubbed sage
2½ tablespoons fresh thyme
4 quarts chicken broth
  Salt and pepper
½ teaspoon cayenne pepper
1 cup minced fresh chives

Melt butter in a large, heavy saucepan over medium heat. Add the onions and sauté until tender, about 10 minutes. Add the squash and sauté until beginning to color, about 10 minutes. Add the sage and thyme and stir 1 minute. Add the broth; bring mixture to boil. Reduce heat and simmer until the squash is tender, about 20 minutes. Transfer the soup to a processor in batches and puree until smooth. Season to taste with the salt, pepper, and cayenne pepper. Ladle the soup into bowls and sprinkle with minced chives.

8 servings

Note: This soup can be prepared a day ahead and kept in a covered bowl in the refrigerator. To reheat, place soup in a saucepan over medium heat for 15 to 20 minutes.

PORK ROULADE WITH PANCETTA, FENNEL, AND PORT WINE SAUCE

Pork Roulade:

1½ tablespoons extra-virgin olive oil, divided

 8 ounces pancetta, chopped

 1 large fennel bulb, trimmed, chopped

 ¼ cup chopped onion

 3 garlic cloves, minced

 6 ounces goat cheese, softened

 ½ cup oil-packed sun-dried tomatoes, drained
   and chopped

 1 (4-pound) boneless center cut pork roast, trimmed
   Twine for securing roast

 1 tablespoon chopped fresh rosemary

 1 teaspoon salt

 1 teaspoon pepper

Preheat the oven to 450 degrees. Heat 1 tablespoon olive oil in a medium sauté pan over medium heat. Add the pancetta, fennel, and onion; sauté 4 minutes. Add the garlic and sauté 1 additional minute. Transfer mixture to a medium bowl to cool. Once the mixture has cooled, add the goat cheese and sun-dried tomatoes and mix well.

Starting off center, slice the pork lengthwise, cutting to—but not through—the other side. Open the butterflied portions, laying the pork flat. Turning knife blade parallel to the surface of a cutting board, slice the larger portion of pork in half horizontally, cutting to—but not through—the other side; open flat. Place plastic wrap over the pork; pound to 1-inch thickness using a meat mallet. *continued on next page* ○

Spread the filling over the pork, leaving a ½-inch margin around the outside edges. Roll up pork, jelly-roll fashion, starting with a long side. Secure at 2-inch intervals with twine.

Combine the rosemary, salt, and pepper. Rub the remaining ½ tablespoon olive oil over the pork. Rub the rosemary mixture into the pork.

Place the pork in a roasting pan and bake at 450 degrees for 20 minutes. Reduce oven temperature to 325 degrees. (Do not remove pork from oven.) Bake an additional 1 hour 15 minutes or until a thermometer registers 150 degrees. Remove pork from the pan, cover, and let stand 15 minutes. Cut pork into ½-inch-thick slices and serve with port wine sauce.

Port Wine Sauce:
 4 cups red wine
 2 cups port wine
 9 tablespoons butter, sliced into tablespoons
   Salt and freshly ground pepper

For the port wine sauce: Combine the wine and port in a large saucepan and bring to a boil over high heat until reduced to 2 cups, about 35 minutes. Lower heat and whisk in the butter. Season with salt and freshly ground pepper.

10 to 12 servings

SPINACH CAKES

3 (10-ounce) packages frozen spinach, thawed, thoroughly drained

4 tablespoons extra-virgin olive oil, divided

2 garlic cloves, minced

½ cup finely chopped onions

1 cup panko bread crumbs

½ cup Parmigiano-Reggiano

2 eggs, beaten

Salt and freshly ground pepper to taste

Place the spinach in a medium bowl. Heat a nonstick skillet over medium heat; add 1 tablespoon olive oil, garlic, and onions and sauté 5 minutes. Add onions and garlic to spinach in the bowl. Add the panko crumbs, Parmigiano-Reggiano, eggs, and salt and pepper to the bowl and mix well. Form mixture into 8 patties.

Heat 3 tablespoons olive oil in a skillet over medium-high heat. Cook the spinach cakes 3 minutes per side.

8 servings

Note: This recipe can be made up to 4 hours ahead. Cover with foil and refrigerate. To serve, preheat oven to 350 degrees and place foil-covered cakes in the oven for 15 minutes, or until warmed through.

APPLE CRUMBLE PIE

Crust:
- 1½ cups all-purpose flour
- ½ teaspoon salt
- 1 stick very cold unsalted butter, cut into small pieces
- ¼ cup ice water

Filling:
- ½ cup sugar
- 2 tablespoons all-purpose flour
- 6 large apples (Jonagold, Rome, or Macoun), peeled, cored, and cut into ½-inch slices
- 2 tablespoons lemon juice

Topping:
- ¼ cup sugar
- 2 tablespoons firmly packed brown sugar
- ½ cup all-purpose flour
- ¾ teaspoon cinnamon
- ¼ teaspoon ground ginger
- ¼ teaspoon freshly ground nutmeg
- ¼ cup unsalted butter

Preheat the oven to 375 degrees.

For the crust: Mix together the flour and salt; using a pastry blender cut the butter into the mixture until crumbly. Add just enough water to form the dough into a ball. Roll out on a lightly floured surface to just over 9 inches in diameter. Place in a pie plate and crimp the edges.

For the filling: Combine the sugar and flour in a large bowl. Add the apple slices and lemon juice, tossing well. Place the apples in the prepared pie crust.

For the topping: Combine the sugar, brown sugar, flour, cinnamon, ginger, and nutmeg. Cut in the butter with a pastry blender until crumbly. Sprinkle the topping over the apples. Cover the edge of pie crust with foil or a crust shield and bake 30 minutes. Remove the foil or crust shield and continue baking another 30 minutes until the pie is golden brown and bubbly.

8 servings

Shopping List

Produce

- 1 garlic bulb
- 30 spears thin asparagus
- 4 large portobello mushrooms
- 10 cups arugula
- 1 lemon
- 1 bunch fresh oregano
- 1 onion

Meat and dairy

- 6 ounces Monterey Jack cheese
- 2 ounces Parmesan cheese
- 3 tablespoons butter
- 8 thin slices prosciutto
- 1½ cups blue cheese
- 6 large eggs
- 2 cups heavy whipping cream

Seafood

- 24 large shrimp
- 16 sea scallops

Bakery

- 1 loaf ciabatta bread
- 1 loaf pumpernickel bread

Other groceries

- Extra-virgin olive oil
- Salt
- Pepper
- Dijon mustard
- Worcestershire sauce
- 2 (28-ounce) cans chopped Roma tomatoes
- Tomato paste
- 1 can capers
- 1 can anchovies
- Red pepper flakes
- 1 pound fettucini
- 7 ounces semisweet chocolate
- Vanilla
- Cream of tartar
- Unflavored gelatin
- Instant espresso powder
- Cinnamon
- Powdered sugar
- Cocoa powder
- Chocolate-covered espresso beans

Plan Ahead

2 days ahead:
Shred cheese

1 day ahead:
Make sauce
Make cake
Blanch asparagus

4 hours ahead:
Sauté prosciutto and asparagus
Whisk dressing
Toast pumpernickel

2 hours ahead:
Grill bread for bruschetta

30 minutes ahead:
Assemble bruschetta and set aside
until ready to pop in the oven

Grilled Bruschetta with Asparagus and Parmesan Cheese

Stacked Portobello Mushroom Salad
with Pumpernickel Crisp and Blue Cheese

Shrimp and Scallops with Light Tomato Caper Sauce and Fettuccini

Espresso Bean Chocolate Roll Cake

We all love a little garlic bread with our pasta, right? With this menu I've put a twist on the bread by adding the asparagus and serving it as an appetizer. The Stacked Portobello Mushroom Salad has a really elegant presentation. You will love all of the Plan Ahead tips in this menu, which make pulling together the final steps a breeze. Don't forget to leave room for dessert—the Espresso Bean Chocolate Roll Cake is truly decadent!

WINE PAIRING: A nice Pinot Noir will complement this menu.

Tip: When trimming asparagus, hold a spear of asparagus horizontally between your hands. Bend the spear, and where the spear breaks you will find the end to trim away. From here you can line up your asparagus and use your first hand-trimmed spear as a template.

GRILLED BRUSCHETTA
WITH ASPARAGUS AND PARMESAN CHEESE

1 loaf ciabatta bread, sliced into 10 (½-inch-thick) slices

1 garlic clove, peeled and halved

2 tablespoons extra-virgin olive oil

Coarse salt and freshly ground pepper

30 spears thin asparagus, tough ends trimmed

6 ounces Monterey Jack cheese, grated

2 ounces Parmesan cheese, grated

Grill bread slices over medium heat until golden brown on both sides. Rub one side of the bread with garlic; brush lightly with oil. Place in a single layer on a baking sheet.

Preheat broiler. Bring a large saucepan of water to a boil over high heat; add a generous pinch of salt. Add the asparagus and cook until tender, 3 to 5 minutes. Drain the asparagus and set aside.

Combine the Monterey Jack and Parmesan in a bowl. Sprinkle two-thirds of the cheese evenly over the ciabatta slices. Arrange 3 asparagus spears on top of each slice. Sprinkle the remaining cheese over the asparagus, dividing evenly. Season with salt and pepper.

Broil until the cheese has melted, 1 to 2 minutes. Remove from oven and cut in half. Serve warm.

10 servings

STACKED PORTOBELLO MUSHROOM SALAD
WITH PUMPERNICKEL CRISP AND BLUE CHEESE

8 (½-inch-thick) slices pumpernickel bread

3 tablespoons butter, melted

¾ cup plus 3 tablespoons extra-virgin olive oil, divided

8 thin slices prosciutto

4 large portobello mushrooms, brushed clean, stems removed, sliced into ½-inch-thick slices

3 garlic cloves, minced

Salt and freshly ground pepper

10 cups arugula

4 tablespoons lemon juice

1½ tablespoons chopped fresh oregano

1 tablespoon Dijon mustard

½ teaspoon Worcestershire sauce

1½ cups crumbled blue cheese

Preheat the oven to 375 degrees. Place pumpernickel slices on a baking sheet. Brush with melted butter and bake 14 minutes in the oven, turning halfway through baking time. Set aside.

Heat 3 tablespoons olive oil in a large sauté pan over medium-high heat. Add the prosciutto and sauté until lightly browned. Add the portobello slices and garlic and sprinkle with salt and freshly ground pepper. Sauté 4 minutes.

Pour the arugula into a shallow salad bowl. Whisk together the lemon juice, oregano, mustard, Worcestershire, and remaining ¾ cup olive oil. Season with salt and freshly ground pepper. Drizzle over the arugula and toss well.

To serve: Divide the arugula evenly among 8 plates. Top with a pumpernickel crisp. Place the mushrooms over each crisp. Top with blue cheese.

8 servings

SHRIMP AND SCALLOPS WITH
LIGHT TOMATO CAPER SAUCE AND FETTUCCINI

Sauce:

¼ cup plus 2 tablespoons extra-virgin olive oil, divided

1 cup finely chopped onion

6 garlic cloves, minced

2 (28-ounce) cans chopped Roma plum tomatoes, with juice

2 tablespoons tomato paste

5 tablespoons drained capers

2 tablespoons minced anchovy fillets

2 tablespoons fresh oregano

½ teaspoon dried crushed red pepper flakes

Salt to taste

24 large shrimp, shelled, deveined

16 sea scallops

1 pound fettuccini, cooked al dente

In a large, heavy saucepan, heat ¼ cup olive oil over medium-high heat. Add the onion and sauté until soft and lightly caramelized, about 6 minutes. Add the garlic and cook an additional 2 minutes. Add the tomatoes, tomato paste, capers, anchovy fillets, oregano, red pepper flakes, and salt. Simmer until the sauce is thickened and slightly reduced, about 30 minutes. Add shrimp to the sauce and mix well. Allow shrimp to simmer in sauce until cooked through, about 4 minutes.

Meanwhile, heat remaining 2 tablespoons olive oil in a large, heavy sauté pan over high heat. Add scallops and sear about 2 minutes per side, until opaque in the center. Add scallops to the sauce and mix well.

Serve over fettuccini.

8 servings

ESPRESSO BEAN CHOCOLATE ROLL CAKE

Cake:

7 ounces semisweet chocolate, chopped

¼ cup water

6 large eggs, separated

⅔ cup sugar, divided

1 teaspoon vanilla

¼ teaspoon salt

¼ teaspoon cream of tartar

For the cake: Preheat the oven to 350 degrees. Line a lightly greased 15 x 10 ½-inch jelly-roll pan with foil and grease the foil. Line the foil with parchment paper and grease the paper. In the top of a double boiler set over barely simmering water, melt the chocolate with ¼ cup water, stirring until the mixture is smooth. Let the mixture cool for 10 minutes.

In a large bowl with an electric mixer, beat the egg yolks with ⅓ cup of the sugar for 5 minutes, or until the mixture is thick and pale. Beat in the cooled chocolate mixture and the vanilla. In another bowl, beat the egg whites with the salt until frothy. Add the cream of tartar, and beat the egg whites until they reach soft peaks. Gradually beat in the remaining sugar until the whites hold stiff peaks. Stir one-fourth of the whites into the chocolate mixture and gently fold in the remaining whites.

Pour the batter into the prepared pan and spread it evenly with a metal spatula. Bake the cake on the middle rack of the oven for 12 to 15 minutes, or until it is puffed and just set. Let the cake cool completely in the pan on a rack. (The cake will be puffed when it comes out of the oven but will sink as it cools.) *continued on next page* ❍

Filling:

1 teaspoon unflavored gelatin
2 tablespoons cold water
1 cup well-chilled heavy whipping cream
2 tablespoons instant espresso powder
⅛ teaspoon cinnamon
¼ cup powdered sugar
4 tablespoons chopped chocolate-covered espresso beans

For the filling: In a small saucepan, sprinkle the gelatin over 2 tablespoons of cold water and let it soften for 5 minutes. Heat the mixture over low heat, stirring until the gelatin is dissolved. Let mixture cool 5 minutes. In a large bowl, combine the cream, espresso powder, and cinnamon, and beat until it holds soft peaks. Add the powdered sugar, and the gelatin mixture. Beat the mixture until it holds stiff peaks. Cover and chill for 10 minutes.

In a small bowl, stir together the cocoa powder and powdered sugar. Sift mixture evenly over the cake. Cover the cake with a piece of parchment paper and invert the cake onto the work surface. Peel off the foil and parchment paper carefully and mound the filling lengthwise down the center of the cake, spreading evenly, leaving a 1-inch border at each end. Sprinkle with chopped chocolate-covered espresso beans. With a long side facing you and using the parchment paper as an aid, roll up the cake jelly-roll fashion, keeping it wrapped in the parchment paper. Chill in the refrigerator while making the glaze.

Glaze:
½ cup heavy whipping cream
¼ cup Kahlúa
1 tablespoon light corn syrup
6 ounces semisweet chocolate, chopped

For the glaze: Bring the whipping cream, Kahlúa, and corn syrup to a simmer in a small saucepan. Remove from heat. Add the chocolate; whisk until smooth. Cool glaze about 10 minutes before using.

Assembly:
3 tablespoons unsweetened cocoa powder
2 tablespoons powdered sugar
3 tablespoons chocolate-covered espresso beans

To serve: Remove cake from parchment paper and place on a serving platter. Slowly pour half of the glaze over the top of the cake, using a cake-decorating spatula (or rubber spatula) to spread the glaze evenly over the top and sides of the cake roll. Pour the remaining glaze over the top of the cake and spread evenly with spatula. In a small bowl combine the cocoa powder and powdered sugar. Line the top of cake with chocolate-covered espresso beans and sprinkle the powdered sugar mixture over the top.

8 servings

Shopping List

Produce
2 to 3 leeks
1 bunch Italian parsley
6 cups baby arugula
1 head radicchio
2 apples, Granny Smith or Macintosh
4 shallots
1 (3- to 4-inch piece) ginger
20 ounces baby spinach

Meat and dairy
6 slices applewood smoked bacon
1 cup Point Reyes blue cheese
2 sticks unsalted butter
4 large eggs
1 pint heavy whipping cream
2 (8-ounce) packages cream cheese

Seafood
32 sea scallops

Other groceries
1 (11-inch) frozen tart shell
Dijon mustard
Kosher salt
Pepper
½ cup sliced almonds
Champagne vinegar
Sugar
Light brown sugar

Egg Beaters
Extra-virgin olive oil
½ cup apple cider
½ cup plus 1 tablespoon pure maple syrup
1 (1-pound) can pumpkin
8 ounces gingersnap cookies
Pumpkin pie spice
Sweetened flaked coconut
½ teaspoon dried thyme

Wine and spirits
1 bottle dry champagne

Plan Ahead

3 days ahead:
Toast almonds for salad

1 day ahead:
Make cheesecake
Make salad dressing

8 hours ahead:
Bake frozen tart shell
Prepare radicchio for salad
Chop shallots for cider sauce
Mince ginger for spinach

2 hours ahead:
Make filling for tart
Bake tart

Applewood Smoked Bacon and Leek Tart

Arugula Salad with Apples, Champagne Mustard Vinaigrette,
and Point Reyes Blue Cheese

Seared Sea Scallops with Cider Glaze

Sautéed Ginger Spinach

Pumpkin Cheesecake in a Gingersnap Crust

While living in California, we loved to hike in Point Reyes National Park. Point Reyes is also home to some pretty lucky Holstein cows that graze on certified organic green pastures overlooking Tomales Bay. Point Reyes Farmstead Cheese Company makes the most amazing blue cheese you will ever taste. You can find their cheese where fine cheese is sold or through the Internet.

WINE PAIRING: A crisp Sauvignon Blanc will do well with this menu.

EQUIPMENT: blender or food processor, 9-inch springform pan with removable bottom

Tip: Purchase "dry packed" scallops, meaning they are shucked from their shell and placed directly into a storage container without the addition of water and preservatives, which plumps them up and makes them impossible to brown.

APPLEWOOD SMOKED BACON AND LEEK TART

1 (11-inch) frozen tart shell
2 tablespoons unsalted butter
4 cups chopped leeks (white and green part)
2 tablespoons Dijon mustard
6 slices applewood smoked bacon, cooked and crumbled
2 eggs
½ cup heavy whipping cream
   Pinch of salt
   Pinch of freshly ground pepper
¼ cup chopped Italian parsley for garnish

Bake the frozen tart shell according to directions on package and allow to cool.

Meanwhile, in a large skillet, melt the butter over medium-low heat; cook leeks, stirring occasionally, for about 30 minutes or until softened. Let cool. Brush the cooled pastry shell with mustard; spread leeks over the top. Sprinkle with bacon. Whisk together the eggs, whipping cream, salt, and pepper; pour over bacon. Bake in 350-degree oven 30 to 35 minutes or until golden brown. Cool 5 minutes; cut into wedges, garnish with parsley, and serve.

8 servings

Michael and Lisa started a supper club three years ago as a means to stay in touch with friends who all used to be neighbors. When their supper club meets, they choose a menu and each couple prepares a segment of the meal and brings it to the host's home for dinner.

We told our supper club about this book, and everyone is very excited to have an organized menu planner.

Each of our five couples took a recipe to prepare. In our house, I do most of the cooking. My husband, Michael, does all of the shopping, bar set up, music selection, and other things that go along with hosting a dinner.

I had never cooked with dry-pack scallops before, but after reading Debi's tip I decided to look for them at our local fish market. I had great results getting the scallops to look and taste restaurant quality.

In these tough economic times, we plan to meet with our supper club more often and save money by not going out to dinner as much.

MICHAEL AND LISA

ARUGULA SALAD WITH APPLES, CHAMPAGNE MUSTARD VINAIGRETTE, AND POINT REYES BLUE CHEESE

Dressing:

3 tablespoons champagne

3 tablespoons champagne vinegar

1 tablespoon sugar

1½ tablespoons Dijon mustard

1 tablespoon pasteurized eggs (Egg Beaters)

1 tablespoon heavy whipping cream

½ teaspoon kosher salt

½ teaspoon freshly ground pepper

⅔ cup extra-virgin olive oil

Salad:

6 cups baby arugula

1 small head radicchio, cut into a chiffonade

2 apples, cored and thinly sliced

½ cup toasted almonds

1 cup crumbled Point Reyes blue cheese

For the dressing: Place all the ingredients in a blender or food processor and blend until smooth. Refrigerate until ready to use.

For the salad: Combine the arugula, radicchio, apples, and toasted almonds in a large salad bowl. Add the desired amount of dressing and toss well. Divide among plates and sprinkle with blue cheese and freshly ground pepper, to taste.

8 servings

SEARED SEA SCALLOPS WITH CIDER GLAZE

4 tablespoons butter, divided
4 tablespoons extra-virgin olive oil
32 sea scallops
   Salt and pepper
½ cup apple cider
½ cup dry champagne
½ cup pure maple syrup
½ cup finely chopped shallots
1 cup heavy whipping cream
½ teaspoon dried thyme

In a large, heavy skillet over high heat, melt 2 tablespoons butter with olive oil. Season the scallops with salt and pepper. Add scallops to the skillet and sauté until cooked through, about 3 minutes per side. Transfer scallops to a platter and tent with foil to keep warm. (Do not clean the skillet.)

Add the cider, champagne, maple syrup, and shallots to the skillet; boil until liquid is reduced to about half. Add 2 tablespoons butter, whipping cream, and thyme. Boil until mixture is reduced to sauce consistency, about 5 minutes. Return scallops to the skillet. Stir until heated through, about 1 minute. Divide the sauce and scallops among plates.

8 servings

SAUTÉED GINGER SPINACH

¼ cup extra-virgin olive oil
⅓ cup minced ginger
20 ounces baby spinach
   Salt and freshly ground pepper to taste

Heat the olive oil in a wok or large skillet over medium-high heat. Add the ginger and sauté 1 minute. Add the spinach and reduce heat to medium-low. Toss the spinach well until just wilted, about 5 minutes. Season to taste with salt and pepper.

8 servings

PUMPKIN CHEESECAKE IN A GINGERSNAP CRUST

Crust:
¼ cup sweetened coconut
8 ounces gingersnap cookies
2 tablespoons sugar
4 tablespoons melted butter

Cheesecake:
2 (8-ounce) packages cream cheese
¾ cup firmly packed brown sugar
2 large eggs
1 (1-pound) can pumpkin
1½ teaspoons pumpkin pie spice
1 tablespoon maple syrup

For the crust: Preheat the oven to 325 degrees. Spread the coconut in a single layer on a baking sheet. Bake 6 to 8 minutes until golden brown. In the bowl of a food processor, place gingersnap cookies and pulse until the cookies are finely crushed. (You will need 1¾ cups.) In a medium bowl, combine the gingersnap crumbs, toasted coconut, sugar, and melted butter. Transfer mixture to a 9-inch springform pan with a removable bottom. Press the crumb mixture about 1 inch up the sides of the pan. Bake the crust until lightly browned, about 15 minutes. Remove the pan from the oven and allow to cool slightly.

For the cheesecake: With an electric mixer, beat together the cream cheese and brown sugar until blended. Add the eggs one at a time, beating well after each addition. Add the pumpkin, pumpkin pie spice, and maple syrup; mix until well blended. Pour mixture into the crust-lined pan.

Bake until the center barely jiggles when the cake is gently shaken, about 50 minutes. Remove from oven and cool on a rack. Cover and chill until cold, at least 2½ hours or up to 24 hours. Run a knife around the edge of the cake and remove the pan sides.

8 to 10 **servings**

Shopping List

Produce

4 shallots
1 garlic bulb
2 pears
1 small bunch celery
3 carrots
4 medium onions
1 small yellow onion
1 bunch green onions
1 bunch Italian parsley
1 bunch fresh thyme
1 bunch fresh rosemary
12 ounces sliced cremini mushrooms
2 pounds green beans
1 lemon

Meat and dairy

3 pounds pork tenderloin
10 ounces Roquefort cheese
1 quart heavy whipping cream
1 pound unsalted butter
1 pint half-and-half
4 cups whole milk
2 large eggs

Seafood

1 pound Phillips lump crab
3 pounds tilapia fillets
¼ pound crab roe

Bakery

15 slices white sandwich bread
1 to 2 loaves challah bread (enough
to make 10 cups)

Other groceries

Extra-virgin olive oil
Ground cinnamon
Pumpkin pie spice
Ground cinnamon
Vanilla extract
Sugar
Bay leaves
11 ounces wild rice
⅓ cup pecans
1½ cups dried apples
All-purpose flour
1 (8-ounce) can water chestnuts
Tabasco sauce
Worcestershire sauce
Whole black peppercorns
Kosher salt
Pepper
Balsamic vinegar
Montreal steak seasoning
1½ cups chicken stock
3½ cups chicken broth
Glazed walnuts
1 (15-ounce) can pure pumpkin
Dark brown sugar
Nonstick cooking spray

Wine and spirits

½ cup white wine
½ cup sherry
1 cup Marsala wine (sweet)

Plan Ahead

2 months ahead:
Make and freeze stock for soup

1 week ahead:
Cut bread for pumpkin bread pudding
into cubes and freeze
Make caramel sauce

1 day ahead:
Make marinade and marinate pork
Start wild rice
Make soup
Wash and trim green beans

8 hours ahead:
Make sauce for pork
Mix cream and cheese

4 hours ahead:
Toast bread

2 hours ahead:
Sauté pears; reserve at room
temperature until assembly
Finish wild rice; rewarm when ready
to serve

Caramelized Pear, Pecan, and Roquefort Toasts

She-Crab Soup with Fresh Snipped Chives

Herb Crusted Pork Tenderloin with Mushroom Marsala Sauce

Wild Rice with Dried Apples and Water Chestnuts

Oven Roasted Green Beans with Shallots and Lemon

Pumpkin Bread Pudding

While visiting South Carolina, it's hard to find a menu without She-Crab Soup—it's a favorite for many. The crab roe used in my recipe may be found frozen in fish markets. Don't worry if you can't find it—the soup will still be delicious. I have given you the recipe for homemade fish stock, which can be made ahead and frozen. You may also take a short cut and use a good quality boxed fish stock, such as Kitchen Basics.

WINE PAIRING: Chardonnay's inherent fullness, creamy texture, and buttery taste make it an ideal companion to this menu.

Tip: When freezing soups, stocks, and sauces, place them in a freezer zip-top bag and lay flat to remove all of the air. This makes for easy storage in your freezer.

CARAMELIZED PEAR, PECAN, AND ROQUEFORT TOASTS

2 tablespoons unsalted butter
2 pears, thinly sliced into wedges
2 teaspoons finely minced shallots
¼ teaspoon ground cinnamon
10 ounces Roquefort cheese
5 tablespoons heavy whipping cream
15 slices white sandwich bread, crusts removed
⅓ cup chopped toasted pecans

Preheat the oven to 350 degrees. Heat a large sauté pan over medium heat. Add butter and sauté pear slices with the shallots and cinnamon until browned, about 7 minutes; remove and set aside. In a small bowl, combine the cheese and heavy whipping cream, mixing well. Cut the bread in half crosswise, making strips 3 x 1½ inches. Transfer the bread slices to a baking sheet; toast in oven until light golden on each side, 10 to 15 minutes. Remove from oven.

Spread a heaping teaspoon of cheese mixture on each bread slice. Top with a few pear slices and sprinkle with toasted pecans. Serve at room temperature.

10 to 12 servings

SHE-CRAB SOUP WITH FRESH SNIPPED CHIVES

2 sticks butter, divided

¼ cup finely chopped onion

¼ cup finely chopped carrot

1 cup finely chopped celery

¾ cup all-purpose flour

2 cups fish stock (see recipe on next page)

4 cups whole milk

2 cups heavy whipping cream

1 pound Phillips lump crab

¼ pound crab roe (optional)

½ cup sherry

1 tablespoon Tabasco

1 tablespoon Worcestershire sauce

Heat a small sauté pan over medium heat. Melt 1 tablespoon butter; add the onion, carrot, and celery and sweat vegetables 3 minutes, stirring frequently. Remove and reserve. In a 7- to 8-quart stockpot, melt the remaining butter. Whisk in flour to make a roux. Continue to whisk as you incorporate the fish stock, milk, and cream. Bring mixture to a boil. Add the crab, roe, sherry, and Tabasco and Worcestershire sauces; reduce heat; and simmer 20 minutes. Adjust with salt and freshly ground pepper.

12 **servings**

Fish Stock

3 pounds tilapia

½ cup white wine

8 cups water

2 medium onions, very thinly sliced

4 stalks celery, very thinly sliced

2 medium carrots, very thinly sliced

2 dried bay leaves

¼ cup roughly chopped Italian parsley

8 sprigs thyme

2 tablespoons black peppercorns

1 teaspoon kosher salt

In a 7- to 8-quart stockpot, combine the fish, white wine, and water. Bring to a boil, skimming off the white foam from the top of the stock as it approaches boiling. Add the remaining ingredients, reduce heat, and simmer gently 20 minutes. Turn off the heat, stir the stock, and steep 10 minutes. Strain through a fine mesh strainer. Refrigerate up to three days, or freeze for up to two months.

Makes 2 quarts

HERB CRUSTED PORK TENDERLOIN
WITH MUSHROOM MARSALA SAUCE

3   pounds pork tenderloin
2   tablespoons balsamic vinegar
2   tablespoons extra-virgin olive oil
3   garlic cloves, crushed
2   tablespoons finely chopped rosemary leaves
2   tablespoons finely chopped thyme leaves
½   tablespoon Montreal steak seasoning
    Mushroom Marsala Sauce (recipe on page 52)

Trim the silver skin or connective tissue from the tenderloin with a very sharp knife.
Place the tenderloin on a nonstick cookie sheet with a rim. Coat the tenderloin with
balsamic vinegar, rubbing vinegar into the meat. Drizzle the tenderloin with olive oil.
Cut small slits into the meat and disperse pieces of crushed garlic into the openings.

Combine the herbs and steak seasoning in a small bowl. Rub the meat with the
mixture. Cover and refrigerate at least 4 hours or overnight.

Allow the meat to sit at room temperature for 1 hour before roasting. Roast in a
500-degree preheated oven for about 20 minutes (until internal temperature reaches
150 degrees). Cover with foil and allow the meat to rest 15 minutes before slicing.
Place slices of pork tenderloin on a plate and spoon the Mushroom Marsala Sauce
over the top.

8 servings

Mushroom Marsala Sauce

- 4 tablespoons unsalted butter
- 12 ounces sliced cremini mushrooms
- 1½ cups chicken stock
- 1 cup Marsala wine (sweet)
- ¾ cup heavy whipping cream
- Salt and freshly ground pepper

Heat the butter in a medium saucepan, add the mushrooms, and sauté about 3 minutes. Remove and reserve the mushrooms. Add the chicken stock to the pan, and over high heat reduce to ½ cup. Add the Marsala and reduce to 1 cup. Add the cream and reduce to 1¾ cups. Return mushrooms to the pan and season with salt and pepper.

Shopping tip: Cremini mushrooms are often labeled as baby bellas.

WILD RICE WITH DRIED APPLES AND WATER CHESTNUTS

1 small yellow onion, chopped
2 tablespoons extra-virgin olive oil
2 cups wild rice (about 11 ounces) rinsed and drained
3½ cups chicken broth
3½ cups water
1½ cups chopped dried apples
¾ cup chopped green onions
1 cup chopped water chestnuts
1 teaspoon salt
½ teaspoon pepper

In a 4- to 5-quart heavy pot over medium heat, cook yellow onions in olive oil, stirring occasionally until golden brown, about 10 minutes. Add the rice and cook, stirring until rice releases a nutty aroma, about 3 minutes. Add the broth, water, and dried apples and bring to a boil, stirring occasionally. Cover and reduce heat. Simmer until the rice is tender (grains will split open), about 1¼ hours. Remove rice from heat and drain well, then return to the pot. Stir in the green onions, water chestnuts, salt, and pepper.

Note: Rice can be cooked (without draining) 1 day ahead. Cool the rice, uncovered; then cover and chill. Reheat rice in a covered pot over low heat, 10 to 15 minutes. Drain before adding the green onions, water chestnuts, salt, and pepper.

8 servings

OVEN ROASTED GREEN BEANS WITH SHALLOTS AND LEMON

2 pounds fresh green beans, trimmed, cut into 2-inch-long pieces

3 shallots, peeled, and cut into thin slivers

4 tablespoons extra-virgin olive oil

1 teaspoon salt

Freshly ground black pepper

½ cup very finely chopped Italian parsley

2 teaspoons lemon zest

Preheat the oven to 425 degrees. Combine the green beans, shallots, olive oil, salt, and pepper in a large bowl. Transfer to a baking sheet and roast 12 to 20 minutes. Toss the roasted beans with chopped parsley and lemon zest.

8 servings

PUMPKIN BREAD PUDDING

  2 cups half-and-half

  1 (15-ounce) can pure pumpkin

  1 cup plus 2 tablespoons firmly packed dark brown sugar

  2 large eggs

1½ teaspoons pumpkin pie spice

1½ teaspoons cinnamon

1½ teaspoons vanilla extract

 10 cups (½-inch cubes) challah bread

    Nonstick cooking spray

    Caramel sauce (recipe on page 57)

    Glazed walnuts, chopped (optional)

Preheat the oven to 350 degrees. In a large bowl use a whisk to blend the half-and-half, pumpkin, brown sugar, eggs, spices, and vanilla. Fold in the bread cubes. Transfer the mixture to a 9 x 13-inch glass baking dish prepared with nonstick cooking spray. Let stand 15 minutes. Bake pudding until a tester inserted into the center comes out clean, about 40 minutes.

Serve with a drizzle of Caramel Sauce and chopped (Emerald brand) glazed walnuts.

Shopping tip: Look for challah bread in the bakery section of your grocery store.

10 servings

Caramel Sauce

1⅓ cups sugar

⅓ cup water

⅔ cup heavy whipping cream

¼ cup unsalted butter, cut into 1-inch pieces

In a large, heavy saucepan over medium-low heat, stir the sugar and water until the sugar dissolves. Increase the heat to high and boil without stirring until the syrup turns deep amber in color. Remove from heat. Add cream. Whisk in butter. The sauce should be served warm.

Note: This sauce can be made up to 1 week ahead of time. Cover and refrigerate until ready to serve. To rewarm, place in a microwave-safe bowl and reheat for 1 minute at 50 percent power, or until heated through.

Shopping List

Produce
1 garlic bulb
1 bunch Italian parsley
1 head frisée
5 red bell peppers
2 medium fennel bulbs
12 cups mixed baby greens
3 lemons
2 large shallots
1 bunch fresh tarragon
1 medium onion
2 large tomatoes
4 apples, Gala or Jonagold
2 lemons

Meat and dairy
6 ounces Spanish chorizo
½ cup Boursin cheese
4 ounces Manchego cheese
6 large eggs
2 tablespoons unsalted butter

Seafood
24 mussels
24 large shrimp
24 medium clams

Bakery
1 loaf ciabatta bread

Other groceries
Extra-virgin olive oil
Kosher salt
Pepper
Red pepper flakes
1 cup bottled clam juice
Saffron threads (about 30)
1½ cups bamba rice or short grain rice
1 teaspoon smoked Spanish paprika
Sugar
1 (14-ounce) can sweetened condensed milk
2 (13-ounce) cans evaporated milk
Vanilla extract
Dark brown sugar
Nutmeg

Wine and spirits
1 cup white wine

Plan Ahead

1 day ahead:
Make broth for paella
Make salad dressing
Roast peppers for salad

8 hours ahead:
Make custard

2 hours ahead:
Sauté apples

1 hour ahead:
Toast bread slices and rub with garlic
Assemble salad and dressing; reserve dressing until ready to toss salad

Crostini with Boursin Cheese, Spanish Chorizo, and Frisée

Roasted Red Pepper, Fennel, and Manchego Cheese Salad

Paella with Clams, Mussels, and Shrimp

Vanilla Custard with Sautéed Apples and Caramel

Paella is a dish that originated in Spain. The ingredients often vary, depending on the chef. Saffron, however, which turns the rice a golden yellow, is one of the key ingredients. Saffron is the stigma of the fall-flowering crocus and must be handpicked, making this labor-intensive spice the most expensive in the world by weight. But by use saffron isn't that expensive. A 1-gram jar is enough to season 2 to 3 large pans of paella. For best results, use a traditional paella pan, which is wide and shallow with handles on the side. In Spain, friends and family gather around the paella pan enjoying conversation and happy memories as their supper cooks. Try my recipe for paella—featuring clams, mussels, and shrimp—at home with your supper club and enjoy a fun evening! ¡Que tengan una noche buena!

WINE PAIRING: Sauvignon Blanc is a good wine choice for the shellfish.

EQUIPMENT: 8 ramekins

Tip: For high quality Spanish ingredients visit www.tienda.com. You can find all of the ingredients you need for this menu, including the bamba rice.

CROSTINI WITH BOURSIN CHEESE, SPANISH CHORIZO, AND FRISÉE

8 (½-inch-thick) slices of ciabatta bread
3 tablespoons extra-virgin olive oil, divided
1 garlic clove, peeled and sliced in half
2 garlic cloves, minced
6 ounces dried Spanish chorizo, thinly sliced
1 tablespoon chopped parsley
½ cup Boursin cheese
1 small head of frisée, tender white and light green leaves only
Salt and freshly ground pepper

Preheat a grill pan. Lightly brush both sides of the bread slices with oil. Grill, turning once, until toasted, about 3 minutes. Transfer the toasts to a platter and rub them with the garlic clove.

In a medium skillet, combine 2 tablespoons olive oil with the minced garlic, chorizo, and parsley. Cook over low heat, stirring occasionally, just until warmed through, about 5 minutes. Spread the Boursin on the toasts and top with the warm chorizo. Garnish with the frisée. Drizzle with the remaining olive oil. Season with salt and pepper.

8 servings

ROASTED RED PEPPER, FENNEL, AND MANCHEGO CHEESE SALAD

4 red bell peppers

¼ cup lemon juice

1 cup extra-virgin olive oil

3 garlic cloves, minced

2 tablespoons chopped shallots

2 tablespoons chopped fresh tarragon

½ teaspoon dried crushed red pepper flakes

½ teaspoon salt

½ teaspoon freshly ground pepper

12 cups mixed baby greens

2 medium fennel bulbs, trimmed, thinly sliced, fronds chopped and reserved

4 ounces Manchego cheese, shaved

Place a sheet of heavy-duty aluminum foil over the top rack in oven. Heat the oven to broil. Place peppers skin-side up on foil and broil until the skin is charred. Remove the foil and peppers from oven; enclose the peppers in foil, 10 minutes. Peel and seed the peppers, then cut into ¾-inch-wide strips.

Whisk the lemon juice, olive oil, garlic, shallots, tarragon, red pepper flakes, salt, and pepper in a medium bowl to blend.

Toss the mixed greens, peppers, and fennel with the desired amount of dressing. Spoon the salad onto plates and garnish with shaved Manchego cheese and the reserved fennel fronds. Season with freshly ground pepper.

8 servings

Note: Peppers and dressing may be made 1 day ahead. Cover separately and chill. Bring dressing to room temperature before using.

PAELLA WITH CLAMS, MUSSELS, AND SHRIMP

24 large shrimp, peeled and deveined, shells reserved

1 cup bottled clam juice

3 cups water

1 cup white wine

1 large pinch of saffron threads (about 30)

¼ cup extra-virgin olive oil

10 garlic cloves, chopped

1 medium onion, coarsely chopped

1 red bell pepper, seeded and chopped

2 large tomatoes, chopped

1 teaspoon smoked Spanish paprika

½ teaspoon kosher salt

Freshly ground black pepper

1½ cups Spanish bamba rice or short grain rice

24 medium clams, such as littleneck, cleaned

24 mussels, debearded and scrubbed clean

1 cup chopped Italian parsley, for garnish

Lemon wedges

Put shrimp shells in a large saucepan placed over medium-high heat and cook, stirring, until they are dry and pink, about 2 to 3 minutes. Add the clam juice, water, wine, and saffron. Bring to a boil over high heat. Reduce heat and simmer 10 minutes. Strain the broth, discarding the shrimp shells.

Heat olive oil in a paella pan or large skillet. Make a sofrito by sautéing the garlic, onion, peppers, tomatoes, and paprika. Cook until the mixture caramelizes a bit and the flavors meld, about 15 minutes. Season with salt and pepper. Fold in the rice, stirring constantly to coat the grains. Increase the heat to high and pour 4¾ cups of the hot broth into the paella pan. Bring the mixture to a boil, stirring the rice to spread evenly in the pan. Reduce to a vigorous simmer, cooking 5 minutes.

Add the clams and mussels, tucking them into the rice. Simmer 10 minutes. Lower the heat to a very gentle simmer and continue to cook 5 minutes. Arrange shrimp in the pan. Continue to cook until the paella looks fluffy and moist, another 5 minutes or so. Remove from heat, cover with foil, and allow to rest 5 to 10 minutes and then garnish with parsley. Serve with lemon wedges.

8 servings

Note: The ideal paella has a toasted rice bottom called socarrat.

VANILLA CUSTARD WITH SAUTÉED APPLES AND CARAMEL

Caramel:
- 1 cup sugar
- ½ teaspoon lemon juice

Custard:
- 6 large eggs
- 1 (14-ounce) can sweetened condensed milk
- 1 (13-ounce) can evaporated milk
- ½ cup sugar
- 1 teaspoon vanilla

Apples:
- 2 tablespoons unsalted butter
- 4 apples, peeled, cored, and cut into 1-inch-thick slices (Gala or Jonagold)
- 1 tablespoon firmly packed dark brown sugar
- A few grinds of freshly ground nutmeg

Preheat the oven to 325 degrees. You will need 8 ramekins and a large baking pan to put them in.

For the caramel: Combine the sugar and lemon juice in a warm pan over medium heat. Constantly stir sugar until it is light brown and becomes caramel, about 12 minutes. Quickly pour approximately 2 to 3 tablespoons of caramel into each ramekin, tilting it to swirl the caramel around the sides. Reheat caramel if it starts to harden.

For the custard: In a mixer or with a whisk, blend the eggs together. Mix in the milks, then slowly mix in ½ cup sugar, and then the vanilla. Blend until smooth after each ingredient is added. Pour the custard into the caramel-lined ramekins. Place the ramekins in a large glass or ceramic baking dish and fill with 1 to 2 inches of hot water. Bake for 45 minutes in the water bath and check with a knife just to the side of the center. If the knife comes out clean, it's ready. Remove ramekins from the oven and the water bath and cool in the refrigerator for 2 hours.

For the apples: Melt the butter in a large skillet over medium-high heat. Add the apples and brown sugar and sauté until the apples are golden brown and the sugar melts and becomes thick like syrup. Finish with the nutmeg.

Presentation: Invert each ramekin onto a small plate; the caramel sauce will flow over the custard. Arrange sautéed apples around each custard.

8 servings

WINTER WONDERFULS

When the cold months of winter are upon us, we move indoors, seeking comfort and warmth. We cover the grill, enjoyed during the warmer months, and turn to braising, roasting, and pan searing. The satisfying flavors of simmering sauces and stews warm our palates and fill our homes with welcoming aromas.

Shopping List

Produce

- 1 lemon
- 1 garlic bulb
- 1 bunch fresh basil
- 2 shallots
- 3 large heads Bibb lettuce
- 10 ounces arugula
- 2 pounds plum tomatoes
- 1 bunch rosemary
- 3 pounds Yukon gold potatoes
- 2 pints fresh raspberries
- 1 bunch mint

Tip: Yukon gold potatoes are excellent for mashed potato recipes because they are rich and creamy. When making mashed potatoes it's important to have the ingredients at room temperature so that they blend easily with the warm potatoes and the potatoes don't become stringy.

Meat and dairy

- 10 ounces thinly sliced prosciutto
- 3 pounds pork tenderloin
- 1 (8-ounce) wheel Brie cheese
- 3 ounces Roquefort cheese
- 1 pound, plus 1 stick unsalted butter
- 1 cup freshly grated Parmesan cheese
- 8 large eggs
- 1 cup milk

Bakery

- 1 French baguette

Other groceries

- 1 cup oil-packed sun-dried tomatoes
- Salt
- Pepper
- ½ cup pine nuts
- ½ cup sliced almonds
- Extra-virgin olive oil
- 1¼ cups dried cranberries
- Sugar
- ⅓ cup red wine vinegar
- 4 tablespoons balsamic vinegar
- 3 (10-ounce) packages frozen raspberries in syrup
- 12 ounces 60% cocoa semisweet chocolate
- 4 ounces unsweetened chocolate
- 1 tablespoon instant espresso powder
- 1 cup firmly packed dark brown sugar
- Raspberry preserves

Wine and spirits

- ½ cup tawny port

Plan Ahead

3 days ahead:
Toast pine nuts
Toast almonds

2 days ahead:
Make raspberry sauce for dessert

1 day ahead:
Make torte
Make sun-dried purée
Remove rind from Brie

8 hours ahead:
Slice tenderloin into medallions
Chop prosciutto

4 hours ahead:
Toast bread for bruschetta

2 hours ahead:
Make dressing
Chop tomatoes

1 hour ahead:
Assemble bruschetta for oven
Prep potatoes and put in saucepan of cool water until ready to cook

Brie, Sun-Dried Tomato, and Basil Bruschetta

Winter Salad with Cranberries, Toasted Almonds,
Roquefort, and Port Wine Dressing

Pork Medallions with Arugula and Tomatoes

Rosemary Parmesan Mashed Potatoes

Chocolate Espresso Torte with Raspberry Sauce

This is the menu I featured in the first cooking class I ever taught. Since moving from California, I sometimes struggled to get the ingredients I was accustomed to finding in the market. I made friends with the produce managers and begged for a regular supply of arugula, cilantro, and chile peppers. These are ingredients that we can now readily find, thanks to the growing popularity of cooking at home. If you have trouble finding an ingredient in your market, ask the store to order it for you. I think you will find your local store very accommodating. If you do have trouble finding fresh arugula, however, fresh spinach may be substituted in the entrée recipe here.

WINE PAIRING: A Pinot Noir, with its vibrant taste and silky texture will add dimension to the lean and tender pork tenderloin.

EQUIPMENT: food processor

BRIE, SUN-DRIED TOMATO, AND BASIL BRUSCHETTA

2 tablespoons extra-virgin olive oil
1 cup oil-packed sun-dried tomatoes, drained, oil reserved
1 teaspoon grated lemon zest
1 garlic clove
¼ teaspoon salt
¼ teaspoon pepper
1 French baguette, sliced into ½-inch-thick slices
1 (8-ounce) wheel Brie cheese, rind removed, sliced into thin slices
½ cup pine nuts, toasted
½ cup chopped fresh basil leaves

Mix together the olive oil and reserved oil from the sun-dried tomatoes. In a food processor, process the sun-dried tomatoes, lemon zest, garlic, salt, and pepper until it forms a paste. Preheat the oven to 375 degrees. Lightly brush both sides of baguette slices with the oil and place on a baking sheet. Bake until just beginning to turn golden brown, about 10 minutes, flipping baguettes halfway through. Spread about 1 teaspoon of the sun-dried tomato paste on each toasted baguette, followed by a slice of Brie, and return to the baking sheet. Bake until Brie is just starting to melt. Remove from the oven and sprinkle with toasted pine nuts and fresh basil.

8 servings

WINTER SALAD WITH CRANBERRIES, TOASTED ALMONDS, ROQUEFORT, AND PORT WINE DRESSING

Dressing:

1¼ cups dried cranberries

½ cup tawny port

⅓ cup plus ¾ teaspoon extra-virgin olive oil, divided

2 shallots, minced

1 garlic clove, minced

⅓ cup red wine vinegar

2 teaspoons sugar

Salt and freshly ground pepper to taste

Salad:

3 large heads Bibb lettuce, torn into bite-sized pieces

½ cup sliced almonds, toasted*

3 ounces Roquefort (about 1 cup), crumbled

For the dressing: Combine cranberries and port in a small heavy saucepan. Bring to a simmer over medium heat. Remove from heat; let stand until the cranberries swell, about 15 minutes.

Meanwhile, in a medium, nonreactive skillet, heat ¾ teaspoon olive oil over medium-high heat. Add the shallots and garlic and sauté about 2 minutes. Add the remaining oil, then vinegar and sugar; stir until the sugar dissolves. Stir in the cranberry mixture. Season with salt and lots of freshly ground pepper.

For the salad: Combine the lettuce and almonds in a large bowl. Add the dressing and toss well. Divide the salad among 8 plates. Top with Roquefort and serve.

8 servings

To toast the almonds, place on a baking sheet and bake in a preheated 350-degree oven until light brown in color, about 6 minutes.

Note: *Dressing may be prepared up to 2 hours ahead. Set aside at room temperature.*

PORK MEDALLIONS WITH ARUGULA AND TOMATOES

⅓ cup plus 2 teaspoons extra-virgin olive oil, divided

10 ounces thinly sliced prosciutto, finely chopped

4 large garlic cloves, minced

3 pounds pork tenderloin, trimmed and sliced crosswise 1-inch thick

4 tablespoons balsamic vinegar

10 ounces arugula, large stems discarded, leaves coarsely chopped

2 pounds plum tomatoes, coarsely chopped

Salt and freshly ground pepper

Heat 1 teaspoon olive oil in a large, nonreactive skillet. Add the prosciutto and garlic and cook over moderate heat, stirring, until the garlic is golden, about 4 minutes. Transfer to a plate.

Add 3 tablespoons olive oil to the skillet. Divide pork medallions into 2 batches. Add the first batch of pork medallions to the skillet and cook over high heat until well browned on the outside and medium inside, 3 to 4 minutes per side. Transfer the first batch of cooked pork to a serving platter and keep warm. Use the remaining olive oil to cook the second batch.

Add the balsamic vinegar to the pan and boil for 1 minute, scraping up any browned bits. Add the arugula and cook, stirring until just wilted, about 2 minutes. Add the tomatoes and the prosciutto mixture. Cook over high heat for 2 minutes, stirring occasionally. Season with salt and pepper. Spoon over the pork medallions and serve.

8 servings

ROSEMARY PARMESAN MASHED POTATOES

3 pounds Yukon gold potatoes, peeled and cut into 1-inch cubes
1 teaspoon salt
1 cup milk, warmed in microwave
1 stick unsalted butter, softened
1 cup freshly grated Parmesan cheese
2 tablespoons finely chopped fresh rosemary
  Salt and freshly ground pepper

In a medium saucepan, cover the potatoes with cold water and stir in 1 teaspoon salt. Bring to a boil over moderately high heat. Boil until the potatoes are tender, about 15 minutes. Drain well and return to the pan. Add the warm milk, butter, Parmesan, and rosemary to the potatoes and mash the mixture with a potato masher. Season with salt and lots of freshly ground pepper.

8 servings

CHOCOLATE ESPRESSO TORTE WITH RASPBERRY SAUCE

This torte is quite rich! You'll have plenty of leftovers for your family to enjoy.

- 1 tablespoon instant espresso powder
- 1 cup water
- 12 ounces 60% cocoa semisweet chocolate, coarsely chopped
- 4 ounces unsweetened chocolate, chopped
- 1 pound (4 sticks) unsalted butter, diced
- 2 tablespoons raspberry preserves

- 1 cup firmly packed dark brown sugar
- 8 large eggs, beaten to blend
  Raspberry Sauce (recipe on page 76)
- 2 pints fresh raspberries
  Mint leaves for garnish

Preheat the oven to 350 degrees. Line the bottom of a 9-inch cake pan with 2-inch-high sides with parchment. Dissolve the instant espresso in 1 cup water. Place all chocolate in a large bowl. Bring the butter, espresso, preserves, and brown sugar to a boil in a medium saucepan, stirring to dissolve the sugar. Add to the chocolate and whisk until smooth. Cool slightly. Whisk in the eggs.

Pour the batter into the prepared pan. Place cake pan into a roasting pan. Pour enough hot water into the roasting pan to come halfway up the sides of the cake pan. Bake until center of the cake is set and a tester inserted into the center comes out with a few moist crumbs attached, about 1 hour. Remove pan from the water. Chill the cake overnight.

To assemble: Allow the torte to sit out of the refrigerator 10 minutes. Run a knife around the outside edge of the pan. Place a platter over the pan. Hold the pan and platter together tightly and invert. Lift off the cake pan and peel off the parchment.

To serve: Pour the raspberry sauce over the torte and garnish the outer edge with fresh raspberries and mint leaves.

Raspberry **Sauce:**

3 (10-ounce) packages frozen raspberries in syrup, thawed
1 tablespoon sugar

Working in batches, puree the raspberries and syrup in a food processor. Strain puree into a medium saucepan; add the sugar and cook over medium heat. Stir until sugar dissolves, about 5 minutes. Cool and refrigerate until ready to serve.

16 servings

Note: Raspberry sauce may be made up to 3 days ahead.

Shopping List

Produce

- 2 shallots
- 1½ pounds cremini mushrooms
- 1 garlic bulb
- 2½ ounces arugula
- 6 cups mixed spring greens
- 1 bunch fresh rosemary
- 1 bunch fresh dill weed
- 1 bunch fresh tarragon
- 1 bunch fresh basil
- 1 bunch Italian parsley
- 1 bunch fresh chives
- 1 lemon
- 1 orange
- 2 pounds (1-inch diameter) beets, red and yellow if available
- 1 large Vidalia onion
- 5 carrots
- 8 ounces fresh shiitake mushrooms
- 3 pounds Yukon gold potatoes
- 3 cups baby spinach

Meat and dairy

- 4 pounds beef chuck (stew beef)
- 12 ounces thick-sliced bacon
- 2 ounces heavy whipping cream
- 1 cup half-and-half
- 1 cup Asiago cheese
- ½ cup Parmesan cheese
- 6 ounces goat cheese, crumbled
- 3 sticks unsalted butter

- 3 (8-ounce) packages cream cheese
- 4 large eggs

Bakery

- 1 French baguette

Other grocery items

- Extra-virgin olive oil
- Kosher salt
- Pepper
- ¾ cup walnuts
- All-purpose flour
- 1 quart beef broth
- 1 (6-ounce) can tomato paste
- Sugar
- 1 package (about 12 ounces) shortbread cookies
- 3 cups mixed frozen berries

Wine and spirits

- 6 tablespoons black raspberry liqueur
- 4 cups red wine

Plan Ahead

1 week ahead:
Cut bread into cubes and freeze
Make chive butter

3 days ahead:
Toast walnuts

2 days ahead:
Make topping and toast bread for crostini

1 day ahead:
Make salad dressing
Roast beets for salad
Make cheesecakes
Make berry sauce

4 hours ahead:
Make beef bourguignon (reheat when ready to serve)

1 hour ahead:
Make potatoes (reheat when ready to serve)
Assemble appetizer for baking

Wild Mushroom and Arugula Crostini

Roasted Baby Beets and Herb Salad
with Goat Cheese and Toasted Walnuts

Beef Bourguignon

Spinach Mashed Potatoes with Chive Butter

Individual Cheesecakes with Mixed Berry Sauce

I really like the way the lemon zest and rosemary add a bit of brightness to the Wild Mushroom and Arugula Crostini–a perfect opener for this menu. The Beef Bourguignon is made with an economical cut of beef, but don't let that fool you– the end result is a luxurious and elegant main course that will melt in your mouth! Individual cheesecakes complete this menu. It's so much fun to have your own personal dessert, and because you bake them in muffin tins, serving them couldn't be easier.

WINE PAIRING: A rich, fruity Merlot will pair nicely with the full and rich flavor of the stew.

EQUIPMENT: food processor

Shopping Tip: When purchasing stew beef look for precut packages, or ask your butcher to cut it for you as a time saver.

WILD MUSHROOM AND ARUGULA CROSTINI

36 (⅓-inch-thick) baguette slices

2 tablespoons extra-virgin olive oil

⅓ cup chopped shallots

5 cups chopped cremini mushrooms (about 1 pound)

2 garlic cloves, minced

2½ ounces arugula, chopped

¼ cup heavy whipping cream

1 teaspoon minced fresh rosemary

1 teaspoon grated lemon peel

Salt and pepper

1 cup grated Asiago cheese

½ cup grated Parmesan cheese

Preheat the oven to 375 degrees. Arrange baguette slices on a baking sheet. Toast in oven until golden, about 9 minutes. Cool.

Heat oil in a large skillet over medium-high heat. Add the shallots and sauté 1 minute. Add the mushrooms and sauté until beginning to brown, about 6 minutes. Stir in the garlic and arugula and sauté 1 minute. Remove from heat. Stir in the cream, rosemary, and lemon peel. Season with salt and pepper. Cool. Mix in both cheeses.

Preheat the oven to 375 degrees. Top each toasted baguette with about 1 tablespoon mushroom topping. Place on 2 baking sheets. Bake until the cheese is melted and beginning to brown, about 10 minutes. Transfer to a serving platter and serve warm.

Makes 36

Note: The baguettes can be toasted up to 2 days ahead. Store in an airtight container at room temperature.

Note: The mushroom and arugula mixture can be prepared up to 2 days ahead. Cover and refrigerate.

This whole menu conjures up snuggling by the fire. The delicious recipe for Beef Bourguignon proves, once again, that no one does comfort food like the French. The potatoes were a tasty change from serving it with buttered noodles. The crostini were a big hit and complemented everyone's choice of before-dinner drink. The lovely little cheesecakes were wonderful and transported easily to the card table where we sometimes like to continue our evening.

What we all loved about this menu is the fact that so much of it could be prepared ahead (and clean-up was so easy) that it freed up more time for us to catch up on our travels and grandchildren.

JACK AND BETTIE

ROASTED BABY BEETS AND HERB SALAD
WITH GOAT CHEESE AND TOASTED WALNUTS

Salad:

- 2 pounds (1-inch diameter) baby beets, red and yellow if available
- Extra-virgin olive oil
- ½ teaspoon kosher salt
- 6 cups mixed spring greens
- 2 cups arugula
- ¼ cup chopped fresh dill weed

- ½ cup chopped fresh basil
- ¼ cup chopped fresh tarragon
- ½ cup chopped Italian parsley
- 6 ounces goat cheese, crumbled
- ¾ cup chopped toasted walnuts
- Vinaigrette (recipe on page 84)

Preheat the oven to 350 degrees. Wash and dry the beets. Trim ends of the beets. Rub the beets with olive oil. Place the beets in a baking dish and sprinkle with kosher salt. Cover the dish tightly with foil. Roast the beets until just tender, about 55 minutes. Cool slightly. Using a towel, rub off the peel from the beets. Slice the beets into ½-inch-thick slices and set aside.

To assemble: Combine the spring greens, arugula, and herbs in a large salad bowl. Add enough vinaigrette to taste and toss well.

To serve: Divide the salad among 8 plates. Top with the sliced roasted beets, goat cheese, and toasted walnuts.

Vinaigrette:

1 teaspoon minced garlic

½ cup lemon juice

½ teaspoon salt

1 teaspoon freshly ground pepper

1 cup extra-virgin olive oil

Whisk together the garlic, lemon juice, salt, and pepper in a small bowl. Gradually whisk in the olive oil.

Note: *The vinaigrette can be made up to 2 hours before your guests arrive.*

8 servings

BEEF BOURGUIGNON

12 ounces thick-sliced bacon, cut into small dice

4 pounds beef chuck (stew beef) cut into 1-inch cubes

1½ cups chopped Vidalia onion

4 tablespoons all-purpose flour

Salt and freshly ground pepper to taste

4 cups red wine

4 cups beef broth

1 (6-ounce) can tomato paste

2½ tablespoons chopped fresh rosemary

5 carrots, peeled and cut into 1-inch-thick slices

2 tablespoons butter

8 ounces fresh shiitake mushrooms, stemmed and thinly sliced

8 ounces cremini mushrooms, quartered

¼ cup chopped fresh Italian parsley

Preheat the oven to 350 degrees. In an ovenproof casserole or Dutch oven, sauté the bacon until crisp. Remove with a slotted spoon and drain on paper towels. Set bacon aside. Pour off all but 3 tablespoons of the bacon drippings.

Over medium-high heat, sauté the beef, stirring frequently, until browned on all sides. Add the onions to the beef, along with the flour, salt, and pepper. Mix thoroughly. Cook over high heat, stirring constantly for about 4 minutes.

Add the wine, beef broth, tomato paste, reserved bacon, rosemary, and carrots. Mix the ingredients together and bring to a boil. Cover the pot and place in preheated oven until the meat is tender, about 2 hours.

Meanwhile melt the butter in a large sauté pan over medium heat. Add the mushrooms and sauté until lightly browned, about 5 to 6 minutes. Remove from the pan and reserve.

When the meat is cooked, transfer the pot to a burner, add the reserved mushrooms and parsley, and heat through on low heat for about 7 minutes. Adjust seasonings with salt and freshly ground pepper to taste.

8 servings

SPINACH MASHED POTATOES WITH CHIVE BUTTER

Chive Butter:

1 stick unsalted butter

¼ cup chopped chives

Potatoes:

3 pounds Yukon gold potatoes, peeled and cut into 1-inch cubes

1 cup half-and-half

4 tablespoons butter

3 tablespoons fresh tarragon or 1½ teaspoons dried tarragon

3 cups chopped baby spinach

Salt and freshly ground pepper to taste

For the chive butter: Place the butter and chives in a food processor and pulse until smooth.

For the potatoes: Cover the potatoes with cold water in a large pot. Bring to a boil; reduce heat and cook until the potatoes are very tender, about 25 minutes.

Meanwhile, combine the half-and-half, butter, and tarragon in a measuring cup. Heat in a microwave for 1 minute. Drain the potato mixture; return to the pot. Add the half-and-half mixture to the potatoes and mash until the vegetables are almost smooth. Season to taste with salt and pepper.

To serve: Top each serving of the mashed potatoes with a pat of the chive butter.

8 servings

INDIVIDUAL CHEESECAKES WITH MIXED BERRY SAUCE

Cheesecakes:

- 2 cups ground shortbread cookies
- ¼ cup unsalted butter, melted
- 3 (8-ounce) packages cream cheese, room temperature
- ¾ cup sugar
- 1 teaspoon grated orange zest
- ¾ teaspoon vanilla extract
- 2 large eggs
- 2 large egg yolks
- Mixed Berry Sauce (recipe on page 88)

Preheat the oven to 325 degrees. Line a 12-cup muffin tin with foil liners. Toss ground cookies with melted butter in a medium bowl to blend. Press 2 tablespoons cookie mixture onto the bottom of each liner, reserving the remaining cookie mixture.

Using an electric mixer, beat the cream cheese, sugar, orange zest, and vanilla in a large bowl until fluffy, occasionally scraping down sides of the bowl, about 1 minute. Add the eggs and yolks 1 at a time, blending well after each addition. Divide the batter equally among foil liners. Sprinkle the reserved cookie mixture evenly atop the batter. Place muffin tin in the oven and bake until cheesecakes are set in the center, about 45 minutes. Remove the cheesecakes from oven and cool completely. Wrap in plastic wrap and refrigerate until cold, about 2 hours.

To serve: Spoon the berry sauce over the cheesecakes.

Makes 12 cheesecakes

Note: Cheesecakes can be made up to 24 hours ahead. Keep refrigerated.

Mixed Berry Sauce:

4 tablespoons unsalted butter

¼ cup sugar

3 cups mixed frozen berries (raspberries, blueberries, blackberries)

6 tablespoons black raspberry liqueur (such as Chambord)

Melt the butter in a heavy medium skillet over high heat. Mix in the sugar. Add the berries and stir until the sugar dissolves and berries are heated through, about 3 minutes. Remove skillet from the heat and stir in liqueur.

Shopping List

Produce

4 onions

1 red onion

1 bunch fresh thyme

1 bunch Italian parsley

1 bunch fresh rosemary

1 garlic bulb

1 bunch fresh basil

8 cups baby spinach

4 cups baby arugula

1½ pounds asparagus

8 ounces cremini mushrooms

4 lemons

1 orange

Meat and dairy

6 ounces prosciutto

4 tablespoons unsalted butter

½ cup blue cheese

1¼ cups Parmigiano-Reggiano cheese

8 eggs

2½ cups milk

2 cups heavy whipping cream

Seafood

1½ pounds U/15 count sea scallops

1 pound large shrimp

Bakery

1 loaf focaccia bread

Other groceries

Kosher salt

Pepper

Canola oil

White truffle oil

Extra-virgin olive oil

Red wine vinegar

½ cup sun-dried tomatoes

2 cups Arborio rice

2 quarts vegetable broth

Sugar

Cake flour

Almond extract

Cornstarch

¾ cup powdered sugar

Wine and spirits

⅓ cup dry red wine

1 cup white wine

½ cup Marsala wine

1 tablespoon rum

2 teaspoons crème de cacao

Plan Ahead

1 day ahead:
Bake cake
Make cake filling

4 hours ahead:
Caramelize onions

2 hours ahead:
Assemble cake

30 minutes ahead:
Assemble focaccia for baking

Toasted Focaccia Bread with Caramelized Onions and Blue Cheese

Asparagus, Spinach, and Crispy Prosciutto Salad

Shrimp and Scallop Risotto with Cremini Mushrooms,
Sun-Dried Tomatoes, and Truffle Oil

Italian Rum Cake with Custard Filling

Have you ever noticed that when you are entertaining, people always tend to hang out in the kitchen? This menu lends itself well to doing just that. It has a nice rustic feel and is perfect for one of those chilly winter nights. While you are in the kitchen, invite one of your friends to help stir the risotto. I think you will find that when everyone helps out people feel at home and more relaxed—after all, isn't that what it's all about?

WINE PAIRING: Chardonnay, with its buttery flavor and creamy texture would be a good match for the risotto.

Tip: Truffles are a hypogenous (underground) version of mushrooms. Because they are difficult to find (in Italy and France they actually use pigs to locate them in the woods), truffles command a very high price tag, at about two hundred dollars per ounce. Thankfully, the wonderful flavor and aroma of truffles can be captured and infused into olive oil at a fraction of the cost. Try drizzling truffle oil into mashed potatoes, on pasta dishes, and even on scrambled eggs. Just remember, a little truffle oil goes a long way. Look for it where you find olive oil in your grocery store. You can also find it in specialty cooking stores or online.

TOASTED FOCACCIA BREAD
WITH CARAMELIZED ONIONS AND BLUE CHEESE

4 tablespoons unsalted butter

3 onions, sliced

2 teaspoons chopped fresh thyme leaves

Kosher salt and freshly ground black pepper

1 loaf focaccia bread

4 tablespoons extra-virgin olive oil

½ cup crumbled blue cheese

½ cup chopped Italian parsley for garnish

Preheat the oven to 400 degrees. Heat the butter in a large skillet over medium heat. Add the onions, thyme, salt, and pepper and cook until the onions are sweet and golden brown, about 20 minutes.

Using a serrated knife, cut the focaccia bread in half lengthwise to make 2 long slices of bread. Brush both sides of each with olive oil.

Place the focaccia slices on a baking sheet and spread with the onions. Place in the oven and bake until the bread is crispy, about 15 minutes. Sprinkle with blue cheese and parsley. Cut into pieces and serve hot.

8 servings

ASPARAGUS, SPINACH, AND CRISPY PROSCIUTTO SALAD

Salad:

- 5 tablespoons extra-virgin olive oil, divided
- 1 small red onion, thinly sliced
- 6 ounces prosciutto, chopped
- 1½ pounds asparagus, trimmed, cut on diagonal into 2-inch pieces
- 8 cups baby spinach
- 4 cups baby arugula
- ½ cup freshly grated Parmigiano-Reggiano cheese
- Red Wine Vinaigrette (recipe on page 94)

In a medium sauté pan heat 2 tablespoons of oil over medium-low heat; add the red onions and cook, stirring occasionally, until they begin to caramelize, about 10 minutes. Transfer to a paper-towel-lined plate to drain.

In a large sauté pan heat 2 tablespoons olive oil over medium-high heat; add the prosciutto and sauté until crisp, about 5 minutes. Using a slotted spoon, transfer to a paper-towel-lined plate to drain. Return the pan to medium-high heat, add an additional tablespoon of olive oil, and sauté the asparagus until tender. Remove from the pan and set aside.

In a large salad bowl, combine the spinach, arugula, asparagus, onions, and prosciutto. Add the red wine vinaigrette a little at a time, tossing well to combine. Garnish with a sprinkle of Parmigiano-Reggiano.

Red Wine Vinaigrette:

¼ cup red wine vinegar

⅓ cup Cabernet Sauvignon or other dry red wine

1 garlic clove, minced

½ cup extra-virgin olive oil

⅓ cup chopped fresh basil

½ teaspoon salt

½ teaspoon freshly ground pepper

In a medium bowl whisk together the vinegar, red wine, and garlic. Slowly add the oil in a steady stream, whisking to emulsify. Stir in the basil, salt, and pepper.

8 servings

SHRIMP AND SCALLOP RISOTTO WITH CREMINI MUSHROOMS, SUN-DRIED TOMATOES, AND TRUFFLE OIL

1 pound large shrimp, shelled and deveined

1½ pounds U/15 count sea scallops

Salt and freshly ground pepper

Canola oil (for searing)

3 tablespoons extra-virgin olive oil

1 small onion, chopped

2 garlic cloves, minced

8 ounces cremini mushrooms, cleaned and sliced

½ cup sun-dried tomatoes

2 cups Arborio rice

1 cup white wine

7 cups vegetable broth, kept at a simmer in a pan on stove

½ cup lemon juice

¾ cup grated Parmegiano-Reggiano cheese

½ cup chopped Italian parsley

1 teaspoon lemon zest

1 teaspoon dried rosemary

3 tablespoons white truffle oil

Heat a very large sauté pan over medium-high heat. Season the shrimp and scallops with salt and pepper. Add just enough oil to cover the bottom of the pan. Once oil is hot, add the scallops to the pan. Be careful to not crowd the pan. Cook in batches if necessary. Sear for 2 minutes on each side. Wipe out the pan and repeat the process with shrimp, cooking shrimp until just pink, 1 to 2 minutes per side. Transfer to a plate and set aside while you make the risotto.

In a large saucepan over medium-high heat add the olive oil; heat, then add the onion, garlic, mushrooms, and sun-dried tomatoes. Sauté until the vegetables begin to soften, about 5 minutes. Add the rice and sauté 1 to 2 minutes, stirring constantly, until the grains begin to look opaque. Add the wine and cook until evaporated.

Add ¾ cup vegetable broth, lemon juice, salt, and pepper. Continue to stir constantly, adding additional stock in ½ cup increments as liquid is absorbed by the rice. Add half of the Parmigiano-Reggiano, parsley, lemon zest, and rosemary.

To serve: Spoon the risotto onto plates and top with the pan-seared shrimp and scallops. Garnish with the remaining cheese and drizzle with truffle oil.

8 servings

ITALIAN RUM CAKE WITH CUSTARD FILLING

Cake:

6 eggs, room temperature, separated
½ cup sugar
1½ teaspoons lemon juice
1½ teaspoons grated orange rind
1 teaspoon almond extract
1 cup cake flour, sifted
½ teaspoon salt

For the cake: Grease and flour an 8-inch round cake pan. Preheat the oven to 350 degrees. Beat the egg yolks until thick and lemon colored. Beat in the sugar, lemon juice, orange rind, and almond extract. Beat until foamy. Fold flour into the egg yolks gently and thoroughly.

Beat the egg whites until foamy and add salt. Beat until stiff. Fold into the egg yolks. Pour the batter into the prepared pan. Bake 45 minutes. Cool. Remove from the pan and cut into four horizontal layers.

To serve: Spread each layer with the custard filling (recipe on page 99) and ice the top and sides with the sweetened whipped cream.

8 servings

Custard Filling:
½ cup sugar
¼ cup cornstarch
   Pinch of salt
2½ cups milk
2 eggs, beaten
1 tablespoon rum
2 teaspoons crème de cacao
½ cup Marsala wine

For the custard filling: Combine the sugar, cornstarch, salt, milk, eggs, rum, crème de cacao, and wine in a saucepan and cook over low heat until thickened. Refrigerate custard until set (about 2 hours).

Sweetened Whipped Cream:
2 cups heavy whipping cream
¾ cup sifted powdered sugar

For the sweetened whipped cream: Combine the whipping cream and powdered sugar in a medium bowl. Beat on high speed using an electric mixer until a stiff peak forms.

Shopping List

Produce

- 1 onion
- 1 garlic bulb
- Fresh ginger (1 [2-inch]) section)
- 1 large carrot
- 2 cups shiitake mushrooms
- 1 bunch fresh cilantro
- 1 bunch green onions
- 3 to 4 limes
- 1 bunch fresh mint
- 10 ounces baby arugula
- 1 pound asparagus
- 1 pint grape tomatoes
- 3 fresh Thai red chiles
- 2 cups baby spinach
- 2 cups curly parsley
- 2 cups fresh basil

Meat and dairy

- 8 thin slices prosciutto
- 8 large eggs
- ¾ cup shaved Asiago cheese
- 3 cups heavy whipping cream

Seafood

- 1 pound lump crab meat
- 3 sea scallops
- 4 medium shrimp
- 16 large shrimp

Bakery

- 2 slices Hawaiian Sweet Bread

Other groceries

- 1 can water chestnuts
- 1 (8-ounce) jar hoisin sauce
- Salt
- Pepper
- 1 (8-ounce) package bean threads
- 1 (16-ounce) package spring roll wrappers
- Canola oil
- Sugar
- Fish sauce
- Unseasoned rice vinegar
- Chile-garlic sauce
- Balsamic vinegar
- Red wine vinegar
- Extra-virgin olive oil
- ¾ cup macadamia nuts
- Turmeric
- 2½ cups panko bread crumbs
- 4 ounces Thai red curry paste
- 3 ounces cream of coconut (such as Cocoa Lopez)
- 4 ounces mango chutney
- 4 ounces pear jelly
- Rice wine vinegar
- 1 (14-ounce) can coconut milk
- Vanilla extract
- 1 cup sweetened flaked coconut
- Turbinado sugar

Plan Ahead

2 weeks ahead:
Make, fry, and freeze spring rolls

1 week ahead:
Make pear vinaigrette
Make Thai chili oil

4 days ahead:
Make Thai curry sauce

3 days ahead:
Make salad dressing

2 days ahead:
Make herb oil

1 day ahead:
Make dip sauce for spring rolls
Make crème brûlée

8 hours ahead:
Roast asparagus

6 hours ahead:
Prepare crab cakes to the step just before frying

4 hours ahead:
Halve tomatoes for salad

2 hours ahead:
Fry crab cakes and keep at room temperature
Reheat on wire rack in oven set over a baking sheet at 375 degrees

Wild Mushroom Spring Rolls with Vietnamese Dipping Sauce

Roasted Asparagus, Tomato, and Arugula Salad

Crab Cakes with Prosciutto Wrapped Shrimp
and Pacific Rim Sauces

Coconut Crème Brûlée

After a few months of winter, I find myself thinking of a vacation, someplace tropical and warm. This menu has a Pacific Rim theme and will definitely get you thinking about Hawaii. Try decorating your table with some black sand (sold in craft stores) and orchids.

WINE PAIRING: a crisp Sauvignon Blanc with citrus tones

EQUIPMENT: food processor, fine mesh sieve, 6-ounce ramekins, deep fryer (optional), wok (optional), crème brûlée blowtorch

Tip: Go to your local craft store and buy squeeze bottles for drizzling sauces. For thicker sauces, you can snip the tops of the bottles to adjust the amount of sauce that comes out. It's a great way to dress up your plate and look like a pro!

WILD MUSHROOM SPRING ROLLS
WITH VIETNAMESE DIPPING SAUCE

1 cup bean threads

2 tablespoons canola oil, plus more for frying the rolls

1 tablespoon minced garlic

1 tablespoon finely chopped ginger

½ cup hoisin sauce

2 cups thinly sliced shiitake mushroom caps

½ cup water chestnuts, finely chopped

½ cup grated carrot

Salt and freshly ground pepper

½ cup chopped fresh cilantro

1 cup chopped green onions

1 (16-ounce) package spring roll wrappers

1 egg beaten with ¼ cup water, for egg wash

In a medium bowl soak bean threads in warm water until soft, 10 to 15 minutes. Drain and cut into 2-inch pieces.

Heat a wok or large skillet over high heat. Add the oil and swirl to coat the pan. When the oil is hot, add the garlic and ginger and cook until soft, about 2 minutes. Reduce the heat to medium, add the hoisin sauce and cook 3 minutes. Add the mushrooms, water chestnuts, and carrot and cook until mushrooms are soft, about 6 minutes. Season with salt and pepper to taste. Transfer the mixture to a medium bowl; add the cilantro, green onions, and bean threads. Stir to blend.

Dampen a kitchen towel. Place 5 spring roll wrappers on a work surface, covering the remainder with the dampened cloth until ready to use. Place about ¼ cup of the filling on the wrappers just above the bottom edge of the wrapper. Fold the bottom edge over the filling and roll halfway; brush the edges with the egg wash, then fold in the sides and continue rolling to enclose the filling completely. Roll as tightly as possible. Cover with the damp cloth and set aside to rest. Fill and roll the remaining wrappers.

continued on next page ◗

Fill a fryer or medium pot one-third full with canola oil and heat to 350 degrees over high heat. Add the spring rolls 4 to 6 at a time and fry until golden, turning as needed, about 5 minutes. Remove rolls with a slotted spoon and drain on paper towels. Slice rolls on the diagonal and serve hot with Vietnamese dipping sauce (recipe below).

Note: Spring rolls may be placed seam side down on a platter covered with the dampened towel and a layer of plastic wrap and refrigerated for up to 4 hours until ready to fry.

Makes 10 rolls

Vietnamese Dipping Sauce:
½ cup fresh lime juice
¼ cup sugar
3 tablespoons fish sauce
1 tablespoon unseasoned rice vinegar
2 teaspoons chile-garlic sauce
2 tablespoons finely chopped fresh mint leaves
1 tablespoon chopped fresh cilantro

In a medium bowl whisk the lime juice, sugar, fish sauce, vinegar, chile-garlic sauce, mint leaves, and cilantro together until the sugar dissolves. Let stand at least 30 minutes.

NOTE: This sauce can be made up to 24 hours ahead. Cover and chill. Allow to reach room temperature before serving.

ROASTED ASPARAGUS, TOMATO, AND ARUGULA SALAD

Cheese-Nut Mix:

¾ cup shaved Asiago cheese

¼ cup finely chopped macadamia nuts

Salad:

1 pound asparagus, trimmed and cut into 2-inch pieces

2 tablespoons extra-virgin olive oil

Salt and pepper

10 ounces baby arugula

1 pint grape tomatoes, sliced in half

For the cheese-nut mix: In a small bowl, combine the Asiago cheese with the Macadamia nuts. Set aside.

For the salad: Preheat the oven to 450 degrees. On a large rimmed baking sheet, toss the asparagus with 2 tablespoons olive oil. Season with salt and pepper and roast 15 minutes, until tender. Set aside to cool.

To assemble the salad: In a large salad bowl combine the arugula, tomatoes, and asparagus. Toss with enough dressing to lightly coat and divide among 8 plates. Top each plate with a sprinkle of the cheese-nut mix.

8 servings

Dressing:

1 garlic clove, minced

3 tablespoons balsamic vinegar

3 tablespoons red wine vinegar

½ teaspoon salt

1 teaspoon freshly ground pepper

1 cup extra-virgin olive oil

For the dressing: Whisk garlic, vinegars, salt, and pepper together in a small bowl. Gradually whisk in olive oil.

CRAB CAKES WITH PROSCIUTTO WRAPPED SHRIMP
AND PACIFIC RIM SAUCES

½ cup macadamia nuts

2½ cups panko bread crumbs

1 pound lump crab meat

½ cup finely chopped sweet onion

1 garlic clove, minced

3 sea scallops, finely chopped

4 medium shrimp, finely chopped

2 slices Hawaiian Sweet Bread, finely chopped

2 ounces heavy whipping cream

2 eggs

1 teaspoon turmeric

4 cups canola oil (for frying)

16 large shrimp, peeled and deveined

8 thin slices prosciutto, cut in half width-wise

¼ cup extra-virgin olive oil

Place macadamia nuts in the bowl of a food processor and pulse until finely chopped. Add panko crumbs and pulse about 5 times to blend. Remove crumb mixture and place in a pie plate. Set aside.

In a large mixing bowl, add the crab, onion, garlic, scallops, medium shrimp, bread, cream, eggs, and turmeric. Mix until well incorporated. Divide the mixture into 8 equal portions, forming into round cakes with your hands. Dredge cakes in the bread crumb mixture, patting to secure crumbs and shape each cake. Place on a parchment-paper-lined baking sheet and continue the process with remaining cakes. Cover the cakes with plastic and refrigerate for at least 1 hour and up to 6 hours to allow the cakes to set.

Heat oil in a deep fryer or large pot to 350 degrees. Fry the cakes a few at a time until golden brown. Drain on paper towels. Set aside. Meanwhile, wrap each large shrimp with a slice of prosciutto and place on a baking sheet. Drizzle with olive oil and bake in a 400-degree preheated oven for about 4 minutes, until shrimp are cooked through. Set aside.   *continued on next page* ❍

To serve: Place 2 tablespoons of Thai Curry Sauce in the center of each plate. Top with a crab cake, and place 2 shrimp on either side of cake. Drizzle Herb Oil around the edge of each plate. Drizzle Mango-Pear Vinaigrette over the crab cakes and plates. Drizzle Thai Dragon Oil over crab cakes and plates.

8 servings

Thai Curry Sauce:

- 4 ounces red Thai curry paste
- ⅓ cup cream of coconut (such as Coco Lopez)
- 2 ounces fresh ginger, chopped
- ½ cup heavy whipping cream
- 4 tablespoons unsalted butter

Place the curry paste, cream of coconut, and ginger in a small saucepan. Bring to a boil over high heat and reduce to medium. Whisk until a smooth paste forms. Add the cream and reduce by half. Add the butter and whisk through. Strain through a fine sieve into a bowl. Warm the sauce slightly before serving.

Note: This sauce may be prepared up to 4 days ahead of time. Cover and refrigerate until ready to use.

Herb Oil:

- 2 cups baby spinach
- 2 cups curly parsley
- 2 cups fresh basil
- ½ cup canola oil
- ½ teaspoon salt
- 1 teaspoon freshly ground pepper

Combine the spinach, parsley, basil, oil, salt, and pepper in a blender or food processor. Blend until smooth. Strain through a fine sieve into a bowl.

Mango-Pear Vinaigrette:
  4 ounces mango chutney
  4 ounces pear jelly
  1 ounce rice vinegar
    Salt and pepper to taste
  2 ounces canola oil

Combine the chutney, jelly, vinegar, and salt and pepper in the bowl of a food processor and process until smooth. With the motor running, slowly add the oil until combined.

Thai Dragon Oil:
  3 fresh Thai red peppers
  4 ounces canola oil

Combine the peppers and oil in the bowl of a food processor and process until smooth. Strain through a fine sieve into a bowl.

Note: If you don't like handling hot peppers, take a short cut and substitute chile oil for the Thai Dragon Oil. You can find chile oil in the Asian foods aisle of your grocery store.

COCONUT CRÈME BRÛLÉE

5 large eggs

¾ cup plus 2 tablespoons sugar

2 cups heavy whipping cream

½ cup coconut milk

1 teaspoon vanilla extract

¼ teaspoon salt

1 cup sweetened flaked coconut, lightly toasted

3 tablespoons turbinado sugar

Preheat the oven to 350 degrees. Position oven rack to the lower third of oven. Whisk together the eggs and sugar until pale in color. Whisk in the cream, coconut milk, vanilla, and salt until combined. Stir in the coconut and pour the mixture into 8 (6-ounce) ramekins. Place the ramekins in a baking pan with 2-inch-high sides. Pour water into the pan to come up halfway on the sides of the ramekins. Bake 30 minutes. Remove the ramekins from the pan and cool to room temperature. Cover and transfer to a refrigerator.

To serve: Sprinkle turbinado sugar evenly over individual ramekins and run a blowtorch over the tops until golden brown. Serve immediately.

Note: *This recipe can be made up to 24 hours in advance.*

8 servings

Shopping List

Produce

½ ounce dried blend shiitake/porcini mushrooms

1 garlic bulb

6 ounces cremini mushrooms

1 bunch fresh thyme

1 bunch fresh rosemary

1 bunch fresh chives

1 (3-inch) piece fresh ginger

2 oranges

2 red bell peppers

2 yellow bell peppers

6 cups mixed field greens

4 pounds Vidalia onions

5 large baking potatoes (such as russet)

2 pints fresh raspberries

Meat and dairy

2 pounds beef tenderloin

1 pound plus 2 tablespoons unsalted butter

5 ounces goat cheese

1½ cups fat-free half-and-half

1⅓ cups heavy whipping cream

6 eggs

Seafood

2 (1½-pound) lobsters

Bakery

1 package dark cocktail rye bread

Other groceries

Kosher salt

Pepper

Dried sage leaves

4 tablespoons miso paste

Rice wine vinegar

Cayenne pepper

Tahini paste

Extra-virgin olive oil

Light brown sugar

Balsamic vinegar

2 cups beef stock

2 tablespoons wasabi paste

½ cup panko (Japanese) bread crumbs

12 ounces Ghirardelli 60% Cacao bittersweet chocolate

Sugar

Vanilla extract

Cake flour

Nonstick cooking spray

Powdered sugar

Wine and spirits

½ cup white wine

¼ cup brandy

6 ounces dark beer

1 tablespoon raspberry liqueur

Plan Ahead

1 day ahead:

Clean and chop lobster

Make salad dressing

Roast peppers

Make mushroom pâté

8 hours ahead:

Make sauce for tenderloin

Make chocolate centers for dessert

3 hours ahead:

Prepare lava cakes and refrigerate until ready to bake

2 hours ahead:

Prep potatoes and assemble

Brandied Wild Mushroom Pâté

Lobster Salad with Roasted Peppers, Miso Dressing, and Goat Cheese

Roasted Beef Tenderloin with Caramelized Onion Sauce

Wasabi Scalloped Potatoes

Individual Chocolate Lava Cakes

When you are ready to splurge, this menu is perfect for that special holiday or celebration dinner. I've updated the "surf and turf" menu of the 1940s supper clubs for today's modern-day supper club. The rich earthy flavor of the wild mushrooms in the pâté will welcome you to the meal. The lobster salad is light and luxurious. Instead of the traditional horseradish sauce you may have found alongside the 1940s "turf" portion of the menu, I have added a modern twist with a bit of wasabi paste to the scalloped potatoes. Dress to match your elegant table and enjoy your celebration!

WINE PAIRING: Sparkling champagne would be a great start. Match the Roasted Beef Tenderloin with a nice Cabernet Sauvignon.

EQUIPMENT: 8 (4-ounce) ramekins, meat thermometer

Tip: Call your seafood store ahead of time and ask them to steam the lobster for you. It will save you time and a pot to wash.

BRANDIED WILD MUSHROOM PÂTÉ

½ ounce dried blend shiitake/porcini mushrooms

1 cup hot water

1 stick unsalted butter

½ cup finely chopped sweet onion (such as Vidalia)

3 garlic cloves, minced

6 ounces cremini (baby bella) mushrooms, sliced

½ tablespoon fresh thyme leaves

½ teaspoon dried sage leaves

1 teaspoon chopped fresh rosemary

½ teaspoon salt

   Freshly ground pepper to taste

½ cup dry white wine

¼ cup brandy

⅓ cup freshly snipped chives for garnish

For the pâté: Soak the dried mushrooms in hot water for 10 minutes, until very tender. Drain well. In a large, heavy skillet melt butter over medium heat. Add the onions and garlic and cook until they begin to soften, about 3 minutes. Add the mushrooms, herbs, salt, and pepper and sauté until very tender. When the liquid begins to evaporate, add the wine and brandy. Reduce until most of the liquid is gone. Cool, taste, and adjust seasonings; then add to a food processor and process until very smooth. Pour into a small bowl or crock and chill until set. Remove from the refrigerator an hour before serving to soften a bit.

To serve: Spread pâté on toasted rye bread and sprinkle with chives.

8 to 10 servings

Rye Toast:

1 package dark cocktail rye bread

4 tablespoons butter, melted (for rye bread toasts)

For the rye toasts: Heat the oven to 350 degrees. Place rye bread squares on a large baking sheet. Bake until lightly toasted on each side. Brush one side with melted butter, return to oven, and bake an additional 3 minutes. Remove from oven and cool.

LOBSTER SALAD WITH ROASTED PEPPERS, MISO DRESSING, AND GOAT CHEESE

Salad:

- 6 cups mixed field greens
- Meat from 2 steamed (1½-pound) lobsters, cut into 1-inch pieces
- 2 red peppers, roasted*, peeled, and cut into ½-inch strips
- 2 yellow peppers, roasted, peeled, and cut into ½-inch strips
- 5 ounces goat cheese, crumbled

For the salad: Place the greens, lobster, and peppers in a salad bowl and add enough dressing to coat. Toss well. Top with sprinkles of goat cheese.

Dressing:

- 4 tablespoons miso paste
- ½ cup rice wine vinegar
- 2 tablespoons ginger
- 2 teaspoons minced garlic
- ½ teaspoon cayenne pepper
- Juice from 2 oranges
- 1 teaspoon tahini

For the dressing: Whisk together the miso paste, vinegar, ginger, garlic, pepper, orange juice, and tahini in a small bowl. Set aside.

*See Roasting technique on page 61.

TIP: *You can find tahini in the Asian section of your grocery store.*

8 servings

ROASTED BEEF TENDERLOIN WITH CARAMELIZED ONION SAUCE

4 tablespoons unsalted butter, divided

16 cups thinly sliced sweet onions, such as Vidalia (about 4 pounds)

2 tablespoons firmly packed light brown sugar

6 ounces dark beer

2 tablespoons balsamic vinegar

2 cups beef stock

1 tablespoon chopped fresh rosemary

Salt and freshly ground pepper to taste

1 (2-pound) beef tenderloin

1 tablespoon extra-virgin olive oil

For the sauce: In a large saucepan melt 2 tablespoons of the butter over medium-high heat. Add the onions and cook, stirring frequently until the onions begin to turn a deep golden brown, about 30 minutes. Add the brown sugar, mix well, and cook 3 minutes. Add the beer and vinegar to the pan, scraping the bottom to loosen browned bits. Cook, stirring occasionally, until mixture is reduced by half. Add the beef stock, mix well, and continue cooking until the sauce is reduced by half. Stir in the rosemary and whisk in the remaining butter. Season with salt and freshly ground pepper.

For the beef tenderloin: Preheat the oven to 350 degrees. Sprinkle the beef generously with salt and freshly ground pepper. In a heavy large skillet heat oil over high heat. Add the beef to the skillet and cook until brown on all sides, about 5 minutes. Transfer the beef to a roasting pan. Roast in oven until a thermometer inserted into center of the beef registers 120 degrees for medium rare, about 35 minutes. Transfer the beef to a cutting board and let rest 10 minutes.

To serve: Cut the beef tenderloin crosswise into ¼-inch-thick slices. Spoon sauce over the slices.

8 servings

WASABI SCALLOPED POTATOES

  1 tablespoon finely chopped ginger
  1 teaspoon salt
  ½ teaspoon freshly ground pepper
 1½ cups fat-free half-and-half
  2 tablespoons prepared wasabi paste
  3 cups (about 5 large) baking potatoes, thinly sliced
  3 tablespoons unsalted butter, cut into small pieces
  ½ cup panko bread crumbs
  3 tablespoons unsalted butter, melted

Preheat oven to 375 degrees. In a medium saucepan, combine the ginger, salt, ground pepper, half-and-half, and wasabi paste. Whisk to blend the ingredients over medium heat until heated through. Spray a 9 x 13-inch glass baking dish with nonstick spray. Layer half of the potatoes over the bottom of the pan. Drop small pieces of butter over the top of the potatoes. Cover with remaining potatoes. Pour the cream mixture from the saucepan over the potatoes. Sprinkle panko bread crumbs over the top and drizzle with the melted butter. Bake for 50 minutes, or until brown and bubbly.

8 servings

INDIVIDUAL CHOCOLATE LAVA CAKES

Centers:

- 3 ounces Ghirardelli 60% Cacao bittersweet chocolate
- ⅓ cup heavy whipping cream

Cakes:

- Nonstick cooking spray
- 6 ounces Ghirardelli 60% Cacao bittersweet chocolate
- 12 tablespoons unsalted butter
- 3 eggs plus 3 egg yolks
- ½ cup sugar
- ¾ teaspoon vanilla
- ⅓ cup cake flour
- 1 tablespoon raspberry-flavored liqueur

Garnish:

- 1 cup heavy whipping cream
- 3 tablespoons powdered sugar
- 8 raspberries

For the centers: Melt chocolate and cream in a double boiler. Whisk gently to blend. Refrigerate about 2 hours or until firm. Form into 6 balls. Refrigerate until needed.

For the cakes: Preheat the oven to 400 degrees. Spray eight 4-ounce ramekins with cooking spray. Melt the chocolate and butter in a double boiler and whisk gently to blend. In a medium bowl, whisk the eggs, yolks, sugar, and vanilla with an electric mixer on high speed, about 5 minutes or until thick and light. Fold the melted chocolate mixture and flour into the egg mixture just until combined. Mix in the raspberry liqueur. Spoon cake batter into the ramekins. Place a chocolate ball in the middle of each ramekin. Bake about 15 minutes or until cake is firm to the touch. Let sit out of the oven for about 5 minutes. Run a small, sharp knife around the inside of each ramekin, place a plate on top, invert and remove ramekin.

To serve: Mix the cream and powdered sugar together in an electric mixer until stiff peeks form. Garnish cakes with raspberries and a dollop of whipped cream.

8 servings

SPRING SPECIALTIES

Spring is a time of renewal as the first blooms appear, the air is fresh, and the days get a little longer. Having that extra bit of daylight is such a treat. When we can squeeze in an after-dinner walk before it gets dark, I know we are on the right track. As we move from winter's slower, more reflective pace, we no longer need that winter coat to keep us warm. Just as easily as we craved those comfort foods we all love, we quickly find we are ready for lighter fare. It's time for refreshing flavors and forward-thinking ideas.

Shopping List

Produce

- 1 large portobello mushroom
- 2 large plum tomatoes
- 1 sweet onion (such as Vidalia)
- 1 bunch fresh basil
- 1 bunch fresh rosemary
- 4 lemons
- 3 garlic bulbs
- 2 to 3 heads Romaine lettuce
- 1 bunch Italian parsley
- 1 bunch fresh oregano
- 2 large fennel bulbs

Meat and dairy

- 8 (4-ounce) skinless, boneless chicken breast halves

- 3½ cups Parmigianno-Reggiano cheese
- ⅓ cup blue cheese
- 1 pound whole milk mozzarella cheese
- 1½ cups salted butter
- 2 sticks unsalted butter
- 5 large eggs
- 1½ pounds cream cheese
- ¼ cup sour cream

Bakery

- 2 French baguettes
- 18 store-bought biscotti

Other groceries

- Extra-virgin olive oil
- Sea salt
- Pepper
- ¾ cup oil-packed sun-dried tomatoes
- 1 (2-ounce) package anchovies
- Garlic powder
- Dried sage leaves
- Dried red pepper flakes
- 1 pound dried orzo pasta
- Sugar
- Cornstarch
- All-purpose flour
- Vanilla extract

Wine and spirits

- ½ cup white wine

Plan Ahead

1 week ahead:
Buy bread for croutons, cut, and freeze

4 days ahead:
Prepare dressing for salad

1 day ahead:
Make marinade for chicken
Marinate chicken bundles
Make cheesecake

8 hours ahead:
Grate cheese for salad
Wash and prep lettuce for salad
Prepare topping for bruschetta
Make croutons

4 hours ahead:
Cut cheesecake into bars
Prepare orzo and keep at room temperature

Portobello Mushroom Bruschetta

Caesar Salad with Parmesan Croutons

Grilled Stuffed Chicken Breasts
with Sun-Dried Tomato Herb Sauce

Citrus Scented Orzo Salad with Fresh Fennel

Lemon Biscotti Cheesecake Bars

I think you will enjoy the balance of lemon, garlic, and cheese in this menu. Did I mention garlic? Don't be afraid of the amount of garlic in the entrée. By cooking the sliced garlic in olive oil over a low flame, you are roasting the garlic, which sweetens and mellows its flavor.

WINE PAIRING: Start with a Chardonnay. When you get to the entrée, a Pinot Noir would work well with the grilled flavor of the chicken.

EQUIPMENT: food processor

Tip: When baking, it is important to use ingredients that are at room temperature to ensure even mixing. If you forget to take your eggs out of the refrigerator ahead of time, to speed things along fill a bowl with hot water. Add your eggs and let sit for 10 minutes. Your eggs will be recipe ready!

PORTOBELLO MUSHROOM BRUSCHETTA

1 tablespoon extra-virgin olive oil

1 large portobello mushroom, chopped into ¼-inch dice

2 large plum tomatoes, seeded and chopped

½ cup oil-packed sun-dried tomatoes

1 cup grated Parmeggiano-Reggiano cheese

⅓ cup crumbled blue cheese

¼ cup minced sweet onion

2 tablespoons fresh chopped basil

1 teaspoon minced fresh rosemary

1 teaspoon grated lemon zest

1 garlic clove, minced

¼ teaspoon freshly ground pepper

1 French baguette sliced into ½-inch-thick slices

In a large, heavy skillet heat olive oil over medium-high heat. Add the mushrooms and sauté until just softened, about 2 minutes. Remove from heat, drain and place mushrooms in a small bowl to cool. Meanwhile, stir together the tomatoes, cheeses, onion, basil, rosemary, lemon zest, garlic, and pepper. Add cooled mushrooms to the mixture and combine well. Arrange baguette slices on a baking sheet; spoon tomato mixture evenly over the slices.

Bake at 350 degrees for 7 to 8 minutes or until cheese melts.

8 servings

CAESAR SALAD WITH PARMESAN CROUTONS

Croutons:

1½ cups salted butter

1 garlic clove, minced

1¼ teaspoons garlic powder

1½ teaspoons dried sage leaves

½ teaspoon sea salt

¼ teaspoon freshly ground pepper

⅓ cup finely grated Parmigiano-Reggiano cheese

1 baguette, sliced into ½-inch pieces

Preheat the oven to 450 degrees. Place butter in a large microwave-safe bowl and microwave about 1 minute or until melted. Add the garlic, dry seasonings, and cheese to the bowl and mix well. Add baguette pieces to the bowl with melted butter mixture all at once and toss well. Spread croutons onto a large baking sheet and bake 15 minutes or until well browned. Allow croutons to cool.

Salad:

8 cups thinly sliced hearts of Romaine lettuce

¾ cup finely shredded Parmigiano-Reggiano cheese

Freshly ground pepper, to taste

Place Romaine and croutons in a large bowl. Add the dressing a little at a time and toss well to combine until salad is well coated. Arrange the salad on plates and garnish with a sprinkling of cheese and freshly ground pepper.

Caesar Dressing:

¾ cup grated Parmigiano-Reggiano cheese

1 (2-ounce) package anchovies, drained

3 medium garlic cloves, minced

½ teaspoon freshly ground pepper

¼ teaspoon salt

¼ cup freshly squeezed lemon juice

1 cup extra-virgin olive oil

Combine the cheese, anchovies, garlic, pepper, salt, and lemon juice in the bowl of a food processor. Blend until smooth. With the processor running, slowly add olive oil. Mix until just blended. Refrigerate until ready to use.

Note: The dressing may be made up to 4 days in advance. Refrigerate until ready to serve.

Note: Croutons may be made up to 24 hours ahead and stored in an airtight container.

Tip: You will only use about half of the dressing and croutons for this recipe. Save the rest for an Italian dinner with the family.

8 servings

GRILLED STUFFED CHICKEN BREASTS
WITH SUN-DRIED TOMATO HERB SAUCE

  1 pound whole milk mozzarella cheese, sliced 1-inch thick
  ¾ cup extra-virgin olive oil
 20 garlic cloves, sliced
  2 tablespoons chopped fresh Italian parsley
  2 tablespoons chopped fresh oregano
  ¼ teaspoon dried red pepper flakes
  8 (4-ounce) skinless, boneless chicken breast halves
  ¼ teaspoon salt plus additional to taste
  ¾ teaspoon pepper plus additional to taste

Place the cheese in a large bowl and set aside. In a medium, heavy skillet heat olive oil over medium heat. Add garlic and sauté until golden, about 4 minutes. Stir in the parsley, oregano, and red pepper flakes. Pour oil mixture over the sliced cheese. Toss gently to coat.

Place each chicken breast half in a gallon-sized freezer bag; pound to thickness of ⅓ inch using a flat heavy mallet or pan. Repeat with remaining chicken breasts. Season with salt and pepper. Place a slice of cheese on 1 breast half. Top with another breast half, aligning large end and pointed ends. Secure with metal or wooden skewers. Repeat with the remaining chicken and cheese. Transfer to a large shallow dish. Pour oil mixture from the cheese over chicken. Cover and refrigerate at least 6 hours or up to 24 hours.

Season the chicken with salt and pepper. Grill over medium-high heat until chicken is just cooked through, about 7 minutes per side. Transfer to plates and keep warm.

....

Sun-Dried Tomato Herb Sauce:

2 tablespoons butter

¼ cup extra-virgin olive oil

8 garlic cloves, sliced

¼ cup oil-packed sun-dried tomatoes, thinly sliced

¼ cup chopped fresh Italian parsley

2 tablespoons chopped fresh oregano

¼ cup chopped fresh basil

2 tablespoons freshly squeezed lemon juice

1 tablespoon lemon zest

½ cup white wine

In a medium, heavy skillet melt the butter with olive oil over medium heat. Add the sliced garlic and sauté until golden, about 3 minutes. Stir in the tomatoes, parsley, oregano, basil, lemon juice, and zest.

For the assembly: Remove skewers from the chicken and cut on the diagonal into 1-inch slices. Pour sauce over the chicken and serve.

8 servings

CITRUS SCENTED ORZO SALAD
WITH FRESH FENNEL

2¾ cups uncooked orzo (about 1 pound)
 ¼ cup extra-virgin olive oil
  2 large fennel bulbs, thinly sliced
  2 teaspoons minced lemon zest
 ¼ cup lemon juice
  1 cup finely grated Parmigiano-Reggiano cheese
     Salt and freshly ground pepper to taste

In a large pot of boiling water, cook orzo according to the package directions. Drain orzo and transfer to a medium bowl. Meanwhile, in a large skillet heat olive oil. Add the fennel and sauté over medium-high heat for 5 minutes. Transfer fennel to the bowl with orzo and toss well with the lemon zest and juice to combine. Allow to cool to room temperature, then add Parmigiano-Reggiano and salt and pepper to taste. Toss and serve.

8 servings

LEMON BISCOTTI CHEESECAKE BARS

Crust:

18 store-bought biscotti

½ cup unsalted butter, melted

⅛ cup sugar

1 teaspoon grated lemon zest

For the crust: Preheat the oven to 325 degrees. Butter a 10-inch square pan. In the bowl of a food processor, add about 18 biscotti and process until crumbs are made. Remove the crumbs, measure out 2½ cups, and return crumbs to the bowl of the food processor. Add the butter, sugar, and lemon zest and process until well combined. Press the crumb mixture evenly over the bottom and ½ inch up the side of the pan. Bake the crust for 8 minutes.

Filling:

1 tablespoon plus 2 teaspoons cornstarch

½ cup cold water

2 large egg yolks

1¾ cups sugar, divided

¼ cup lemon juice

1 teaspoon finely grated lemon zest

1¼ pounds cream cheese, softened

2 tablespoons all-purpose flour

3 large eggs, at room temperature

¼ cup sour cream

1 teaspoon pure vanilla extract

For the filling: In a small bowl, dissolve cornstarch in the water. In a medium saucepan, whisk the egg yolks with ¾ cup of the sugar and the lemon juice. Whisk in the cornstarch mixture and cook over moderate heat, whisking gently, until the sugar is dissolved and the lemon mixture is hot, about 4 minutes. Boil over moderately high heat for 1 minute, whisking constantly, until the mixture is thick and glossy. Transfer the lemon mixture to a heatproof bowl. Stir in the lemon zest and let cool.

In a large bowl, using an electric mixer, beat the cream cheese with the remaining 1 cup of sugar until smooth. Beat in the flour until blended. Add the eggs one at a time, beating well between additions. Add the sour cream and the vanilla and beat until the batter is smooth.

For the assembly: Pour the cream cheese batter over the crust and smooth the surface with a spatula. Dollop the lemon mixture on the cheesecake batter and carefully swirl into the batter using a sharp knife. Bake the cheesecake for about 40 minutes or until golden around the edges and just set. Run the tip of a knife around the edge to loosen the cheesecake from the side of the pan. Let cool on a wire rack 1 hour, then refrigerate the cheesecake at least 6 hours or overnight. Cut into 16 bars and serve.

Note: *This recipe may be prepared and refrigerated up to 3 days before serving.*

Makes 16 bars

Shopping List

Produce

1 package alfalfa sprouts

1 lemon

1 English cucumber

4 bunches green onions

1 (3-inch) piece fresh ginger

8 limes

1 head Napa cabbage

1 head radicchio

1 red bell pepper

1 yellow bell pepper

1 jalapeño

1 large carrot

1 bunch fresh cilantro

1 bunch fresh mint

1½ pounds russet potatoes

1 garlic bulb

2 kiwi

1 pint raspberries

1 pint blueberries

12 large strawberries

Meat and dairy

1 (5½-pound) boneless pork shoulder

½ cup sour cream

14 eggs

½ cup unsalted butter

Seafood

8 ounces smoked salmon

Other groceries

1 package won ton wrappers (found in the produce section of your grocery store and at Asian markets)

1 teaspoon wasabi paste

Extra-virgin olive oil

8 ounces hoisin sauce

Whole black peppercorns

16 mu shu pancakes (purchase from a Chinese restaurant the day of your dinner)

½ cup rice vinegar

Soy sauce

Sesame oil

Creamy peanut butter

1 can water chestnuts

Canola oil

Sesame seeds

Nonstick cooking spray

1¼ cups shelled pistachios

2 cups macadamia nuts

½ cup graham cracker crumbs

½ cup firmly packed golden brown sugar

½ cup sweetened coconut flakes

1 (10-ounce) bag frozen blackberries

Wine and spirits

¼ cup brandy

Plan Ahead

1 month ahead:

Make won tons and freeze

1 day ahead:

Make tartlet crusts

Make curd

Roast and shred pork

Make blackberry sauce

Make wasabi cream

Make dressing for slaw

8 hours ahead:

Prep all ingredients for slaw

Assemble tarts

6 hours ahead:

Make crispy potato cakes

1 hour ahead:

Toss slaw

Crispy Won Tons with Smoked Salmon and Wasabi Cream

Slow Roasted Hoisin Glazed Pork Roast

Asian Slaw

Crispy Potato Cakes

Fresh Fruit Tartlets with Pistachio Coconut Crust
and Blackberry Drizzle

The elegant Crispy Won Tons with Smoked Salmon and Wasabi Cream are designed to pop in your mouth in just one bite. The wasabi crème is just right with the crunch of the shell and the cucumber. You will love how simple the Hoisin Glazed Pork is to prepare. Your friends and you will experience a nice blend of Asian flavors and finish with a delicious delicate fruit tartlet.

WINE PAIRING: A Riesling would be a good choice for this menu.

EQUIPMENT: food processor, mini-muffin tin, crockpot, 8 (4-inch diameter) tartlet pans with removable bottoms

Tip: Russet potatoes are a firm medium starch potato with a weblike structure that makes them perfect for the Crispy Potato Cakes.

CRISPY WON TONS WITH SMOKED SALMON AND WASABI CREAM

1 package won ton wrappers
½ cup sour cream
¾ tablespoon lemon juice
1 teaspoon wasabi paste
8 ounces smoked salmon, thinly sliced
1 package alfalfa sprouts
½ English cucumber, julienned

For the won ton shells: Preheat the oven to 350 degrees. Trim the won ton wrappers to form 2-inch squares. Coat a nonstick mini-muffin tin with cooking spray and press a won ton square into each cup. Lightly coat the squares with cooking spray and bake for about 7 minutes or until lightly browned. Repeat the process with the remaining wrappers.

For the wasabi cream: In a small bowl mix the sour cream, lemon juice, and wasabi paste together.

To serve: Spoon ¼ teaspoon of the wasabi cream into the bottom of the cup. Starting at one short side, roll a slice of salmon into a rosette. Place salmon on top of wasabi cream and garnish with the sprouts and cucumber. Repeat with the remaining won tons.

Note: The won ton shells may be prepared up to 1 week ahead of time if stored in an airtight container in a cabinet or up to 1 month ahead if placed in freezer bags and stored in the freezer.

8 to 10 servings

SLOW ROASTED HOISIN GLAZED PORK ROAST

1 tablespoon extra-virgin olive oil

1 (5½-pound) boneless pork shoulder

1 cup bottled hoisin sauce

3 bunches green onions, cut on diagonal into 1-inch pieces (about 6 cups)

1 teaspoon whole black peppercorns

¼ cup brandy

¾ cup water

Sliced green onions for garnish

16 mu shu pancakes*

Preheat the oven to 300 degrees. In a large, heavy ovenproof pot heat oil over high heat. Add pork shoulder, fat side down; brown on all sides, turning often, about 12 minutes. Remove the pot from heat. Spread hoisin sauce over the pork; sprinkle with the green onions and peppercorns. Cover the pot and place in the oven. Cook until pork is very tender when pierced with a fork, about 2¾ hours, adding water by ¼ cups if mixture is dry.

Remove the pot from the oven. Transfer pork to a cutting board and tent with foil. Let pork stand 20 minutes.

Meanwhile, spoon off fat from pan juices. Stir the brandy and ¾ cup water into juices; boil until the sauce has reduced a bit.

Using two forks, shred the pork. Add pork to the sauce and mix well. Let cool. Refrigerate overnight. Transfer the mixture to a crockpot set on low. Cook 4 hours. Garnish with green onions.

To serve: Spoon pork into the center of each mu shu pancake and roll up like a burrito.

Purchase the mu shu pancakes from your favorite Chinese restaurant the day of the dinner.

8 servings

ASIAN SLAW

Slaw:
- 1 head Napa cabbage, thinly sliced
- ½ head radicchio, thinly sliced
- 1 red bell pepper, julienned
- 1 yellow bell pepper, julienned
- ½ jalepeño pepper, minced
- 1 large carrot, grated
- 2 green onions, thinly sliced
- ½ cup chopped fresh cilantro
- 4 tablespoons mint leaves, thinly sliced
- ½ teaspoon freshly ground pepper

For the slaw: In a large bowl combine the cabbage, radicchio, peppers, carrot, green onions, cilantro, mint, and ground pepper together. Add dressing and toss well.

Dressing:
- 3 tablespoons minced ginger
- ½ cup rice vinegar
- 1 tablespoon soy sauce
  Juice of 1 lime
- 2 tablespoons sesame oil
- ½ cup creamy peanut butter

For the dressing: In the bowl of a food processor, combine the ginger, vinegar, soy sauce, lime juice, sesame oil, and peanut butter. Process until well blended.

8 servings

CRISPY POTATO CAKES

1½ pounds russet potatoes (about 3 medium), unpeeled and scrubbed

½ cup thinly sliced green onions

¼ cup chopped fresh cilantro

2 garlic cloves, minced

2 teaspoons minced peeled fresh ginger

¾ teaspoon salt

¼ teaspoon freshly ground pepper

1 large egg

1 tablespoon sesame oil

3 tablespoons sesame seeds

5 tablespoons canola oil

½ cup finely chopped water chestnuts

¼ cup finely chopped red bell pepper

In a large saucepan of boiling salted water cook the potatoes until tender when pierced with a knife, about 40 minutes. Drain and cool slightly. Peel the potatoes. Cut the potatoes into large pieces and place in a medium bowl. Add the green onions, cilantro, garlic, ginger, salt, and pepper; mash potatoes until well blended. Mix in the egg. Add sesame oil. Form potato mixture into eight 2¾-inch-diameter patties, each about ¾-inch thick. Place the potato cakes on a platter.

Sprinkle both sides of cakes with sesame seeds. Heat canola oil in a large skillet over medium-high heat. Working in batches, add potato cakes to the skillet and cook until golden brown, about 3 minutes per side.

Note: Cakes can be prepared up to 6 hours ahead. Cover with plastic wrap and refrigerate until ready to use.

8 servings

FRESH FRUIT TARTLETS WITH PISTACHIO COCONUT CRUST AND BLACKBERRY DRIZZLE

Lime Curd:

1 cup sugar

¾ cup fresh lime juice

10 large egg yolks

½ cup chilled unsalted butter, cut into pieces

For the lime curd: In a large bowl whisk the sugar, lime juice, and egg yolks together until blended. Set the bowl over a saucepan of simmering water–do not allow the bottom of the bowl to touch the water–and whisk constantly until the mixture thickens, about 9 minutes. Remove bowl from heat. Gradually add butter, whisking until melted and well blended. Press plastic wrap directly on surface of the curd. Refrigerate until cold, about 3 hours.

Crusts:

Nonstick cooking spray

1¼ cups shelled pistachios (about 5 ounces)

2 cups macadamia nuts (about 7 ounces)

½ cup sweetened coconut flakes

½ cup firmly packed golden brown sugar

½ cup graham cracker crumbs

3 large egg whites

For the crusts: Preheat the oven to 350 degrees. Spray eight 4-inch-diameter tartlet pans with removable bottoms with nonstick cooking spray. Combine the nuts, coconut, brown sugar, and graham cracker crumbs in a food processor. Process until the nuts are finely chopped. Transfer to a large bowl. In another bowl beat the egg whites until soft peaks form. Fold whites into the nut mixture in 3 batches (mixture will be sticky). Let mixture stand 10 minutes. *continued on next page* ❍

Using plastic wrap as an aid, press about ⅓ cup nut mixture onto the bottoms and up the sides of each prepared pan. Place the pans on a baking sheet. Bake until crusts are puffed and beginning to brown, about 20 minutes. Cool crusts in pans 5 minutes. Using an oven mitt, gently remove the pan sides. Cool crusts completely on a wire rack.

Blackberry Sauce:
   1 (10-ounce) bag frozen blackberries

For the sauce: Purée the blackberries in a processor until smooth. Transfer to sieve over a small bowl and push the sauce through with the back of a spoon in order to catch the seeds. Transfer blackberry sauce to a squeeze bottle.

Topping:
   2 kiwi fruits, peeled, thinly sliced
   1 pint raspberries
   1 pint blueberries
  12 large strawberries, hulled, thinly sliced

To serve: Fill each crust with some of the lime curd. Arrange the fruit decoratively over curd. Place tartlet on a plate and drizzle with blackberry sauce.

Makes 8 tartlets

Note: The lime curd can be prepared up to 24 hours ahead and kept in the refrigerator.

Note: Crusts can be prepared up to 24 hours ahead. Store in an airtight container at room temperature.

Shopping List

Produce

- 1 bunch fresh basil
- 2 poblano peppers
- 5 limes
- 2 bunches fresh cilantro
- 2 heads Romaine lettuce
- 1 large and 1 medium red onion
- 2 ears corn
- 1 large tomato
- 1 garlic bulb
- 1 bunch green onions
- 1 red bell pepper
- 1 yellow bell pepper
- 1 jalapeño pepper
- 2 ruby red grapefruit
- 1 avocado
- 1 sweet onion (such as Vidalia)

Dairy

- ¾ cup Parmesan cheese
- 12 ounces Pepper Jack cheese
- 1 (16-ounce) container sour cream
- ½ cup crumbled feta cheese
- 1 stick unsalted butter
- 5 large eggs
- 1 cup milk
- 1½ cups heavy whipping cream

Seafood

- 8 (6-ounce) pieces halibut

Other groceries

- 3 (6-ounce) jars marinated artichoke hearts
- 8 (8- to 10-inch) flour tortillas
- 4 corn tortillas
- 1 can chipotle chiles in adobo sauce
- Dijon mustard
- Ground coriander
- Extra-virgin olive oil
- Kosher salt
- Pepper
- ½ cup shelled, toasted pumpkin seeds
- Canola oil
- ¾ cup orange juice
- ⅓ cup soy sauce
- ¼ cup grapefruit juice
- 1 teaspoon dried sage leaves
- 1 teaspoon dried oregano
- 1 (4-ounce) can green chiles
- 2 cups basmati rice
- Sugar
- Vanilla extract
- All-purpose flour
- Baking powder
- Ground cinnamon
- 1 cup semisweet chocolate chips
- 1 (14-ounce) can sweetened condensed milk
- 1 (12-ounce) can evaporated milk
- Powdered sugar
- 2 tablespoons hot chocolate mix
- 1 jar fine quality caramel sauce

Wine and spirits

- ⅓ cup tequila
- ⅓ cup triple sec

Plan Ahead

4 days ahead:
Make marinade for fish

3 days ahead:
Toast pumpkin seeds
Make salad dressing

1 day ahead:
Cook tortilla strips
Make cake
Prepare rice to stage just before baking, cover, and refrigerate

Morning the day of:
Purchase fish

6 hours ahead:
Make relish
Cook corn and remove kernels
Chop tomatoes

Artichoke Quesadillas

Southwestern Caesar Salad

Tequila Marinated Halibut with Grapefruit Avocado Relish

Creamy Green Chile Rice

Chocolate Tres Leches Cake

When I made these Artichoke Quesadillas for my cooking classes, they flew off the plate. I know several people from my classes made this entire menu with their supper clubs and really loved it. The Southwestern Caesar Salad features crispy tortilla strips in place of traditional croutons for a unique crunch. The Creamy Green Chile Rice has just the right amount of cool to balance the Grapefruit Avocado Relish.

WINE PAIRING: The crisp, clean and almost spicy flavor of a Pinot Blanc would be great with this menu.

Tip: When purchasing fresh fish, you should smell the ocean air and nothing fishy. Find a good fish market where the fish is flown in daily and is moved along quickly.

ARTICHOKE QUESADILLAS

¾ cup basil leaves

3 (6-ounce) jars marinated artichoke hearts, drained

¾ cup grated Parmesan cheese

8 (8- or 10-inch) flour tortillas

2 cups grated Pepper Jack cheese

2 poblano peppers, roasted*, peeled,
   and cut into thin strips

   Extra-virgin olive oil

Stack 5 to 6 basil leaves on top of one another. Starting from the top of the leaf, roll the stack into a tight bundle. Using a sharp knife, cut into thin strips.

In the bowl of a food processor combine the artichoke hearts, Parmesan, and basil chiffonade and pulse to finely chop. Place 1 tortilla on work surface. Spread one-fourth of the artichoke mixture on the tortilla. Sprinkle with grated Pepper Jack cheese and some of the poblano strips. Place second tortilla over the top and press gently. Repeat process with the remaining ingredients.

Heat a large, nonstick skillet or griddle over medium-high heat and brush with olive oil. Place quesadillas in the pan and cook until one side is lightly browned, about 2 minutes. Turn each quesadilla over and cook until golden, about 2 or 3 minutes more. Remove from the pan and cut into wedges.

*See roasting technique on page 61.

8 servings

SOUTHWESTERN CAESAR SALAD

Salad:

3 tablespoons extra-virgin olive oil

1 large red onion, thinly sliced

¼ cup canola oil (for frying tortilla strips)

4 corn tortillas, cut into thin strips

2 heads Romaine lettuce, washed and torn into pieces

1 large tomato, chopped

½ cup toasted pumpkin seeds

½ cup crumbled feta cheese

   Kernels from 1 ear of cooked corn

For the salad: In a large skillet heat olive oil over medium-low heat. Add the red onions and cook, stirring often until browned and caramelized, about 20 minutes. Remove and drain on paper towels.

In a medium skillet heat canola oil over medium-high heat. Add tortilla strips and fry until crisp; drain on paper towels.

To serve: Place the lettuce, tomatoes, pumpkin seeds, feta cheese, and corn in a salad bowl. Add dressing and toss to combine. Divide the salad among plates and top with crispy tortilla strips.   *continued on next page* ◐

Dressing:

- 2 teaspoons chopped chipotle chiles in adobo sauce
- 3 garlic cloves
- 2 tablespoons sour cream
- 1 tablespoon Dijon mustard
- Juice of 2 limes
- ½ cup chopped fresh cilantro
- ½ teaspoon ground coriander
- Salt and freshly ground pepper to taste
- ½ cup extra-virgin olive oil

For the dressing: Combine the chiles, garlic, sour cream, mustard, lime juice, cilantro, coriander, and salt and pepper in a blender. Gradually add in the olive oil until smooth.

Shortcup Tip: Purchase an individual serving of microwavable corn in the freezer section of your grocery store and save a few minutes and a dirty saucepan.

8 servings

TEQUILA MARINATED HALIBUT
WITH GRAPEFRUIT AVOCADO RELISH

3   garlic cloves
3   green onions
⅓   cup tequila
⅓   cup lime juice
⅓   cup triple sec
⅓   cup orange juice
⅓   cup soy sauce
¾   cup extra-virgin olive oil
8   (6-ounce) pieces of halibut
    Grapefruit Avocado Relish (recipe on page 154)

Prepare the marinade: Combine the garlic, onions, tequila, lime juice, triple sec, orange juice, and soy sauce in a food processor. Slowly drizzle the olive oil in and blend until smooth. Transfer to a glass jar.

Place halibut in a zip-top bag. Add enough marinade to cover. Refrigerate and marinate for 30 minutes.

For the halibut: Preheat a slightly oiled grill pan over medium-high heat. Pat the halibut dry with a paper towel and cook until just barely firm to the touch, 3 to 4 minutes per side. Transfer the cooked fish to plates and top with Grapefruit Avocado Relish.

Grapefruit Avocado Relish

- ¼ cup extra-virgin olive oil
- ½ medium red onion, finely diced
- ¼ cup finely diced red bell pepper
- ¼ cup finely diced yellow bell pepper
- 1 to 2 tablespoons jalapeño peppers, seeded and minced
- ¼ cup orange juice
- ¼ cup grapefruit juice
- 1 teaspoon kosher salt
- ½ teaspoon sugar
- 2 ruby red grapefruits, peeled and segmented
- 1 avocado, peeled, seeded, and chopped
- ¼ cup chopped fresh cilantro

In a heavy saucepan heat the olive oil. Add the onions, peppers, and jalapeño and cook for a few minutes, until they just begin to soften. Add the juices, salt, and sugar and heat through. Add the grapefruit sections, avocado, and cilantro, tossing well to combine. Adjust seasonings with salt and pepper. Set aside.

8 servings

CREAMY GREEN CHILE RICE

3 cups water

3 teaspoons extra-virgin olive oil, divided

1 teaspoon kosher salt

1 teaspoon sage

1 teaspoon dried oregano

2 cups basmati rice

½ cup chopped Vidalia onion

2 garlic cloves, minced

1 (4-ounce) can chopped green chiles

1¼ cups sour cream

1 teaspoon salt

1 tablespoon lime juice

Kernels from 1 cooked ear of corn

¼ cup chopped fresh cilantro

In a large, heavy saucepan bring the water, 1 teaspoon of the olive oil, salt, and herbs to a boil. Add the rice, stir, cover, and bring back to a boil. Reduce the heat to low and simmer until the moisture is gone, about 15 minutes. Turn off the heat and steam covered for 10 minutes. Fluff with a fork and turn into a large bowl to cool a bit.

Meanwhile, in a medium skillet sauté the onion, garlic, and chiles with the remaining 2 teaspoons of olive oil. Transfer to the bowl with rice.

In a medium bowl combine the sour cream with salt and lime juice. Add the sour cream mixture, corn, and cilantro, to the rice and mix well to combine. Transfer to an oiled baking pan. Cover with foil and bake at 350 degrees until heated through, about 20 minutes.

8 servings

CHOCOLATE TRES LECHES CAKE

½ cup unsalted butter

1 cup sugar

5 large eggs

1½ teaspoons vanilla extract, divided

1 cup semisweet chocolate chips, melted and cooled

1½ cups all-purpose flour

½ teaspoon ground cinnamon

1½ teaspoons baking powder

1 cup milk

1 (14-ounce) can sweetened condensed milk

1 (12-ounce) can evaporated milk

1½ cups heavy whipping cream

¼ cup powdered sugar

2 tablespoons powdered hot chocolate mix

1 jar caramel sauce, warmed

Preheat the oven to 350 degrees. Grease and flour a 13 x 9-inch baking dish. Set aside.

With an electric mixer beat the butter and sugar at medium speed until fluffy; mix in the eggs and 1 teaspoon vanilla extract. Add the melted chocolate and mix until combined. In a small bowl combine the flour, cinnamon, and baking powder; add gradually to butter mixture, stirring to blend. Pour the batter into prepared dish, and bake for 30 minutes or until a wooden toothpick inserted in the center comes out clean. Pierce the cake all over with a fork.

In a large bowl combine the milk, condensed milk, and evaporated milk, and pour on top of the cake. Cool to room temperature. Cover and refrigerate until well chilled, at least 4 hours or overnight.

With an electric mixer beat the whipping cream, powdered sugar, hot chocolate mix, and remaining vanilla at medium-high speed until stiff peaks form; spread over the cake. Cut cake into squares and drizzle with the warmed caramel sauce.

16 servings

Shopping List

Produce

- 2 garlic bulbs
- 6 limes
- 1 (5-inch) piece of fresh ginger
- 2 stems fresh lemon grass
- 1 bunch fresh cilantro
- 4 large plum tomatoes
- 6 small Japanese eggplants
- 1 orange
- 2 large apples, such as Granny Smith
- 2 large pears, such as D'Anjou

Meat and dairy

- 2½ pounds pork tenderloin
- 2 pounds boneless, skinless chicken thighs
- 5 tablespoons unsalted butter
- 1½ cups heavy whipping cream
- 2 quarts vanilla ice cream

Seafood

- 2 pounds large shrimp

Wine and spirits

- 1½ cups dry white wine

From the Asian aisle in your grocery store or Asian market

- 1 cup bottled teriyaki sauce
- Soy sauce
- 6 tablespoons fish sauce
- 2 (11-ounce) cans straw mushrooms
- Peanut oil
- Yellow miso
- Thai red curry paste
- Jasmine rice
- 1 (14-ounce) can pure coconut milk

Other groceries

- Brown sugar
- 1 cup creamy peanut butter
- 36 bamboo skewers
- 2 quarts chicken broth
- Red pepper flakes
- Sugar
- Salt
- ½ cup sweetened coconut flakes
- All-purpose flour
- Baking powder
- ¼ cup candied (crystallized) ginger
- 3 cups dried fruit (a mix of currants, dried cranberries, dried blueberries, dried apricots)
- 1 cinnamon stick
- 3 tablespoons vegetable shortening

Plan Ahead

3 days ahead:
Make peanut dipping sauce

1 day ahead:
Make marinade for pork

8 hours ahead:
Slice pork
Peel and devein shrimp
Poach fruit

4 hours ahead:
Prepare chicken and vegetables for stir-fry
Bake shortcakes

2 hours ahead:
Marinate pork
Make rice

30 minutes ahead:
Skewer and grill pork

Pork Satay with Peanut Dipping Sauce

Thai Hot and Sour Soup

Chicken and Japanese Eggplant Stir-Fry with Garlic and Chiles

Coconut Jasmine Rice

Ginger Shortcakes with Spiced Poached Fruit
and Vanilla Ice Cream

You can find all of the ingredients for these recipes at most grocery stores. Or for a different shopping experience, check your phone book for an Asian market near you. I love to visit the market near our house with my daughters. We always find something new and interesting to try. Not only will you find all of the ingredients, you can also find inexpensive Asian-inspired dishware for your table. And don't forget the chopsticks!

WINE PAIRING: To complement the ginger and other Asian flavors, try pairing this menu with a Riesling.

EQUIPMENT: wok, 36 bamboo skewers, parchment paper

Tip: When purchasing ginger, look for a piece with skin that is smooth and tight. Use a vegetable peeler to peel the ginger.

PORK SATAY WITH PEANUT DIPPING SAUCE

1 cup bottled teriyaki sauce

4 garlic cloves, minced

3 tablespoons fresh lime juice

2½ tablespoons minced fresh ginger

2 tablespoons firmly packed brown sugar

2½ pounds pork tenderloin, cut into ½-inch-wide strips

36 bamboo skewers

Peanut Dipping Sauce (recipe on page 161}

Combine the teriyaki sauce, garlic, lime juice, ginger, and brown sugar in a large glass baking dish. Stir until sugar dissolves. Add the pork and stir to coat. Cover and chill 30 minutes to 2 hours.

Meanwhile, soak bamboo skewers for at least 30 minutes. Thread pork slices onto skewers. Preheat grill over medium-high heat and grill skewers about 3 minutes per side, or until cooked through. Serve with Peanut Dipping Sauce.

8 to 10 servings

Peanut Dipping Sauce:

1   cup creamy peanut butter

1   (14½-ounce) can chicken broth

¼   cup fresh lime juice

3   tablespoons firmly packed brown sugar

2   tablespoons plus 1 teaspoon soy sauce

2   tablespoons chopped peeled fresh ginger

½   teaspoon dried crushed red pepper flakes

For the sauce: Place peanut butter in a heavy medium saucepan. Gradually mix in the chicken broth. Add the lime juice, brown sugar, soy sauce, ginger, and red pepper. Stir over medium heat until smooth and thick, about 6 minutes.

Note: *The Peanut Dipping Sauce can be prepared up to 3 days ahead. Cover and refrigerate. Before serving, stir over medium heat until hot, thinning with water if necessary.*

THAI HOT AND SOUR SOUP

6 cups chicken broth

2 pounds large shrimp, peeled and deveined

1 teaspoon dried red pepper flakes

2 stems lemon grass, cut into 1-inch sections

1 cup chopped fresh cilantro

8 tablespoons lime juice

6 tablespoons fish sauce

2 (11-ounce) cans straw mushrooms

4 large plum tomatoes, chopped

Heat the broth to boiling. Add the shrimp, red pepper flakes, lemon grass, cilantro, lime juice, fish sauce, mushrooms, and tomatoes. Reduce to medium heat and cook only until shrimp turn pink and begin to curl, about 2 minutes. Remove from heat and serve.

8 Servings

CHICKEN AND JAPANESE EGGPLANT STIR-FRY WITH GARLIC AND CHILES

½ cup peanut oil, divided

2 tablespoons minced fresh ginger, divided

2 pounds boneless, skinless chicken thighs, cut into ½-inch-thick slices

1½ tablespoons yellow miso (fermented soybean paste)

⅔ cup water

6 small Japanese eggplants, unpeeled, cut into 3-inch-long, ½-inch-wide strips

2 tablespoons minced garlic

2 tablespoons soy sauce

2 teaspoons Thai red curry paste

In a wok or large, heavy skillet heat ¼ cup of the oil over high heat until hot. Add ½ tablespoon of the ginger to the oil and stir-fry 30 seconds. Add the chicken and continue to stir-fry until cooked through, about 5 minutes.

Remove chicken from the wok and set aside. In a small bowl mix the miso and water. Set aside.

Add remaining oil to the wok and heat until hot. Add eggplant strips and toss to coat with the oil. Stir-fry until strips are lightly browned and tender, about 3 minutes. Add the garlic and remaining ginger. Stir-fry 10 seconds. Add the miso mixture, soy sauce, and curry paste and stir until liquid thickens, about 30 seconds. Transfer to a large bowl and serve.

8 servings

COCONUT JASMINE RICE

1 (14-ounce) can pure coconut milk (regular or light)
1½ cups water
1 teaspoon sugar
  Pinch of salt
1½ cups jasmine rice

Garnish:
  Toasted shredded coconut
  Chopped fresh cilantro

In a medium saucepan combine the coconut milk, water, sugar, and salt. Stir until sugar is dissolved and the ingredients are well blended. Stir in the jasmine rice and mix well. Bring to a boil over medium heat. Cover tightly, reduce heat, and simmer 18 to 20 minutes.

To serve: Sprinkle rice with the toasted coconut and chopped cilantro.

8 servings

GINGER SHORTCAKES WITH SPICED POACHED FRUIT AND VANILLA ICE CREAM

Shortcakes:

  3 cups all-purpose flour

1½ tablespoons baking powder

½ cup sugar

¼ cup chopped candied (crystallized) ginger

  3 tablespoons shortening

  3 tablespoons unsalted butter

1½ cups heavy whipping cream, divided

  2 quarts vanilla ice cream

For the shortcakes: Preheat the oven to 375 degrees. In a medium bowl combine the flour, baking powder, sugar, and ginger. Cut in the shortening and butter. Mix in the heavy whipping cream with a wooden spoon until just combined. Set remaining whipping cream aside. Turn out onto a lightly floured work surface and knead gently 3 or 4 strokes. Pat out until the dough is about 1-inch thick. Cut into 12 rounds and place on a parchment-paper-lined baking sheet. Brush with reserved cream and sprinkle with sugar. Bake until golden brown, about 10 minutes.

Spiced Poached Fruit:

- 1 cup simple syrup (see below)
- 3 cups dried fruit (a mix of currants, dried cranberries, dried blueberries, dried apricots)
- 1½ cups dry white wine
- 1 large piece of orange peel
- 1 cinnamon stick
- 2 tablespoons butter
- 1½ cups peeled and sliced apples, such as Granny Smith
- 1½ cups sliced pears, such as D'Anjou, (skins on)
- 2 tablespoons sugar

To make the simple syrup: In a medium saucepan stir together ½ cup sugar with ½ cup water over medium heat until sugar dissolves.

For the fruit: Combine dried fruit, wine, orange peel, cinnamon, and simple syrup in a medium saucepan over medium-high heat. Bring to a slow boil, then reduce heat to medium and simmer 15 minutes to soften the fruit.

Meanwhile, in a large skillet melt butter over medium-high heat. Add the apples, pears, and sugar, and sauté until fruit is golden brown, about 5 minutes. Add to the poached fruit mixture, stirring to combine.

To serve: Slice each shortcake in half horizontally and place the bottom half on a plate. Spoon some of the poached fruit onto shortcake. Place the top half on the fruit mixture. Serve a scoop of vanilla ice cream alongside the shortcake.

12 servings

Shopping List

Produce

3 bunches fresh cilantro
1 garlic bulb
1 pound tomatillos
1 small white onion
1 serrano chile
9 fresh poblano chiles
1 lime
3 medium onions
2 large yellow onions
1 head Romaine lettuce
1 red bell pepper
1 green bell pepper
4 Roma tomatoes

Meat and dairy

1 prepared rotisserie chicken
24 ounces Monterey Jack cheese
1 cup heavy whipping cream
½ cup sour cream
½ cup milk
1 egg
2 sticks unsalted butter
1 cup half-and-half

Seafood

24 large uncooked shrimp
1 (16-ounce) container Phillips brand lump crab meat

Other groceries

Extra-virgin olive oil
Ground cumin
Chipotle chile powder or cayenne pepper
3 (7-ounce) cans Herdez brand salsa verde
Salt
Pepper
4½ cups chicken broth
Corn oil
Mexican oregano
1 dozen corn tortillas
3 teaspoons annatto seeds
2 cups long grain rice
4 (14.5-ounce) cans black beans
All-purpose flour
Sugar
1 (.25-ounce) package active dry yeast
Ground cinnamon
Blue corn tortilla chips

Plan Ahead

3 days ahead:
Make enchilada sauce

2 days ahead:
Grate cheese for enchiladas

1 day ahead:
Make tomatillo dipping sauce
Roast poblanos for dip
Make beans (reheat when ready to serve)
Shred chicken for enchiladas

12 hours ahead:
Make cookies

4 hours ahead:
Assemble enchiladas up to the step of adding the cream

Note: if making ahead, add less sauce when assembling; add remaining sauce when ready to go into the oven.

2 hours ahead:
Make rice and cover pan to keep warm
Marinate shrimp

1 hour ahead:
Make crab dip and transfer to chafing dish
Grill shrimp

Cilantro Shrimp Skewers with Tomatillo Dipping Sauce

Crab and Poblano Chile con Queso

Chicken Enchilada Suizas

Yellow Rice

Black Beans with Peppers and Tomatoes

Cinnamon Sugar Cookie Crisps

My earlier cooking classes featured this menu and it was very popular. Several students have made the recipes over and over again. Decorate your table with cacti in small terra cotta pots and with colorful candles. It's a casual yet festive menu that I think you will love!

WINE PAIRING: Serve with ice cold Mexican beer and margaritas.

EQUIPMENT: chafing dish, bamboo skewers

Tip: This would be a perfect menu to try with your supper club for Cinco de Mayo, a Mexican holiday that has become popular here in the United States.

CILANTRO SHRIMP SKEWERS WITH TOMATILLO DIPPING SAUCE

1 cup extra-virgin olive oil

½ cup chopped fresh cilantro

4 garlic cloves, minced

2 teaspoons ground cumin

½ teaspoon chipotle chile powder (or cayenne pepper)

24 large uncooked shrimp, shelled and deveined

Wooden skewers

In a medium bowl combine the olive oil, cilantro, garlic, cumin and chile powder. Add the shrimp and marinate in the refrigerator for 1 hour.

Meanwhile, soak wooden skewers in hot water for 30 minutes. Thread 4 shrimp onto each skewer. Grill over medium heat, 2 minutes per side. Serve with Tomatillo Dipping Sauce.

Tomatillo Dipping Sauce:

1 pound fresh green tomatillos, husked

3 tablespoons finely chopped white onion

1 serrano chile, finely chopped

Juice of 1 lime

1 bunch fresh cilantro, roughly chopped

½ cup sour cream

In a large pot of boiling water blanch the tomatillos for 15 seconds. Remove the tomatillos from the pot and place in a large bowl of cold water for 5 to 7 minutes.

In the bowl of a food processor add the onion, chile, lime juice, cilantro, sour cream, and tomatillos. Process until smooth.

8 servings

CRAB AND POBLANO CHILE CON QUESO

4 tablespoons vegetable oil

1 medium onion, minced

4 garlic cloves, minced

3 poblano chile peppers, roasted, seeded, peeled, and chopped

4 cups Monterey Jack cheese, shredded

1 (16-ounce) can Phillips lump crab meat

1 cup half-and-half

Salt

Blue corn chips

In a large, heavy skillet heat oil over medium-low heat. Add the onion and garlic and sauté until the onion is softened. Add the poblano chile peppers, cheese, crab, and the half-and-half. Cook over low heat, stirring constantly until the cheese is creamy, about 5 minutes. Season to taste with salt. Transfer to a heated chafing dish and serve immediately, along with blue corn chips.

Makes 4 cups (12 to 16 servings)

CHICKEN ENCHILADA SUIZAS

Filling:

1 prepared rotisserie chicken
1 teaspoon Mexican oregano
½ teaspoon salt

For the filling: Remove the skin from the chicken and discard. Remove all the meat from the chicken and shred using two forks. In a medium bowl combine the shredded chicken, oregano, and salt. Toss to combine and set aside.

Sauce:

6 poblano chiles, roasted, peeled, seeded, and chopped
3 (7-ounce) cans Herdez brand salsa verde
½ yellow onion, chopped
2 garlic cloves, chopped
3 leaves Romaine lettuce, torn
¼ cup chopped fresh cilantro
1½ teaspoons salt
1½ cups chicken broth, divided
2 tablespoons corn oil

For the sauce: In a blender or food processor place the chiles, salsa verde, onion, garlic, lettuce, cilantro, salt, and ½ cup chicken broth. Blend to a smooth purée. In a skillet heat 2 tablespoons corn oil, add purée, and cook over medium heat for 3 minutes, stirring constantly. Slowly stir in the remaining chicken broth and cook until sauce thickens, 5 to 10 minutes. Keep warm in a skillet on the stove. *continued on next page* ❍

Assembly:

6 teaspoons corn oil, divided

12 corn tortillas

8 ounces Monterey Jack cheese, grated

1 cup whipping cream

2 tablespoons chopped fresh cilantro (optional)

To assemble: Preheat the oven to 350 degrees. In a 9 x 13-inch glass baking dish add 1 ladle of the prepared sauce and spread evenly over the bottom. Set aside. In a small nonstick skillet heat ½ teaspoon corn oil over medium-high heat. Add 1 corn tortilla and cook a few seconds; flip and cook a few seconds on the other side. Using tongs, remove the corn tortilla and dip each side in the skillet of warm sauce to coat well. Transfer tortilla to the baking dish. Place some of the prepared filling across the middle of the tortilla, fold one edge over, and roll to close. Place seam side down in baking dish. Repeat this process with the remaining 11 tortillas.

Spoon the remaining sauce over the enchiladas, paying particular attention to coating the ends. Sprinkle the shredded Monterey Jack cheese over the enchiladas and cover evenly with the whipping cream. Bake uncovered for 15 to 20 minutes.

Garnish with chopped cilantro.

8 servings

YELLOW RICE

3 tablespoons canola oil

3 teaspoons annatto seeds

2 cups long grain rice

½ medium onion, chopped

1 garlic clove, minced

3 cups chicken broth

1 teaspoon salt

In a medium saucepan preheat oil and fry annatto seeds over low heat. When the seeds turn dark brown and the oil is dark orange, remove the seeds from the oil and discard. Add the rice to the oil and sauté 5 minutes. Add the onion and garlic and cook until soft. Add the chicken broth and salt to the rice. Bring mixture to a boil, reduce heat to low, and cook until liquid is absorbed, 20 to 25 minutes.

8 servings

BLACK BEANS WITH PEPPERS AND TOMATOES

    2 tablespoons extra-virgin olive oil
    1 medium onion, chopped
    1 red bell pepper, seeded and chopped
    1 green bell pepper, seeded and chopped
    3 cloves garlic, minced
    ½ teaspoon salt
    4 (14.5-ounce) cans black beans, rinsed and drained
 1½ tablespoons ground cumin
    ¼ teaspoon cayenne pepper (add more if you like spicy)
    ½ teaspoon Mexican oregano
    ½ teaspoon freshly ground pepper
    4 Roma tomatoes, chopped
    ¾ cup chopped fresh cilantro
    1 tablespoon unsalted butter

In a large skillet heat olive oil over medium heat. Add the onions, peppers, garlic, and salt. Cook until the vegetables are softened, about 5 minutes. Add the black beans, stirring to combine. Add the cumin, cayenne pepper, oregano, ground pepper, tomatoes, and cilantro. Cook until heated through, just a couple of minutes. Add the butter and mix well. Adjust the seasoning with salt and pepper.

8 servings

CINNAMON SUGAR COOKIE CRISPS

1 (.25-ounce) package active dry yeast
¼ cup warm water
2 cups all-purpose flour
¾ cup plus 1½ tablespoons sugar, divided
½ teaspoon salt

½ cup unsalted butter
½ cup milk, scalded and cooled
1 egg yolk
2 teaspoons ground cinnamon
4 tablespoons unsalted butter, melted

In a small bowl mix the yeast with warm water and set aside to soften. Meanwhile, sift together the flour, 1½ tablespoons sugar, and salt in a large bowl. Cut in the butter using a pastry blender or two forks until only small crumbles remain. Combine the milk, egg yolk, and softened yeast in a small bowl and add to the flour mixture. Mix well. Cover the bowl with plastic wrap and refrigerate for at least 2 hours.

Preheat the oven to 400 degrees.

In a small bowl mix together ¾ cup sugar with the cinnamon and set aside.

Place the dough on a lightly floured cutting board and knead for about 1 minute. Roll out into a 10 x 18-inch rectangle and brush with the melted butter. Sprinkle three-fourths of the cinnamon-sugar mixture evenly over the buttered dough. Beginning at one 18-inch side, roll dough jelly-roll-style to close. Cut roll into 1¼-inch slices and place on an ungreased cookie sheet. Gently press slices to flatten out a bit. Brush tops of all slices with melted butter and sprinkle with the remaining cinnamon-sugar mixture. Bake 12 to 15 minutes, until golden brown. Cool on wire racks.

Makes 15 to 18 cookies

We used Debi's Mexican menu and had a sign-up sheet for each couple to choose a recipe that appealed to them. We are all very busy with young children, so being able to share the cooking responsibilities for a dinner like this is the only way we can do it!

Each couple prepared an item from the menu and brought it to our house. We decorated our table with Mexican glassware and candles. We sipped margaritas and enjoyed spicy salsa and homemade salty chips (that we added to the menu). Each couple brought to the table the experience of cooking with their spouse. One neighbor said she never would have made homemade chips if it had not been for our supper club.

The enchiladas were spicy and something very different for a lot of our neighbors here in rural upstate New York. It was a wonderful way to escape our day-to-day lives and pretend we were away in Mexico for the evening.

Thanks, Debi. We love your menus and cannot wait to try more.

TOM AND TRACEY

SUMMER SENSATIONS

I really enjoy the summer months. The farmers' market returns, which means fresh local produce, cheese, and other local findings. I love to plan a meal around what is fresh and in season. Summer offers us so many wonderful choices. Because this can also be a busy time of year, I like to create recipes that can be started in the morning and completed when I return after a busy day. The menus that follow will take you outside to the grill. Enjoy the season and all it has to offer.

Shopping List

Produce

2 garlic bulbs
1 red bell pepper
1 yellow pepper
2 poblano peppers
6 green onions
1 bunch basil
2 bunches Italian parsley
2 avocados
2 ears of corn
1 pound tomatillos
6 jalapeños
3 bunches fresh cilantro
2 limes
10 ounces mixed field greens
3½ cups grape tomatoes
1 bunch fresh oregano
2 pounds small red-skinned potatoes
1 small Vidalia onion
6 cups blueberries
1 lemon

Meat and dairy

2½ pounds tri-tip steaks
1 cup crumbled feta cheese
½ cup buttermilk
½ gallon vanilla ice cream
¾ cup unsalted butter
5 tablespoons milk

Seafood

¾ pound shrimp

Bakery

1 French baguette

Other groceries

1 (15-ounce) can black beans
   Extra-virgin olive oil (at least 2½ cups)
   Salt
   Pepper
   Rice vinegar
8 corn tortillas
   Vegetable oil
   Mayonnaise
   Ground cumin
   Ground coriander
   Cayenne pepper
1 (14-ounce) can hearts of palm
3 cups mesquite wood smoke chips
1 (8-inch) square disposable aluminum foil baking pan
   All-purpose flour
   Ground cinnamon
   Nutmeg
   Sugar

Plan Ahead

2 days ahead:
Make vinaigrette

1 day ahead:
Fry tortilla strips
Make marinade for steak
Make chimichurri sauce
Make dressing for potato salad

8 hours ahead:
Make blueberry pie
Prep and assemble potato salad (toss with dressing 1 hour ahead)

6 hours ahead:
Toast baguette rounds
Make bruschetta topping and refrigerate

2 hours ahead:
Marinate steaks

Shrimp, Avocado, and Black Bean Bruschetta

Mixed Greens with Crispy Tortillas
and Jalapeño Vinaigrette

Mesquite Grilled Steak with Chimichurri Sauce

Southwestern Potato Salad

Blueberry Pie à la Mode

Chimichurri sauce originated in Argentina as a sauce for grilled meats. It is simple to make and adds an amazing dimension to the charred flavor of a great steak. I add just a bit of jalapeño to my chimichurri, which my brother-in-law Tom absolutely loves. I think you will too.

WINE PAIRING: Serve a Zinfandel to match some of the spicy flavors found in this menu.

EQUIPMENT: food processor, 3 cups mesquite wood smoke chips (found in hardware and cooking stores), 1 (8-inch) square disposable aluminum baking pan

Tip: Tomatillos are a fruit that should not be confused with an unripe green tomato. The tomatillo is in the tomato family, but part of a different generation. The tomatillo grows inside a papery husk and should be firm and bright green in color to ensure freshness. Tomatillos are the base for many Latin green sauces and can be found in most grocery stores today.

SHRIMP, AVOCADO, AND BLACK BEAN BRUSCHETTA

2 tablespoons extra-virgin olive oil

¾ pound shrimp, peeled, deveined, and chopped

4 garlic cloves, minced

½ red bell pepper, diced

½ yellow bell pepper, diced

1 poblano pepper, diced

6 green onions, chopped

1 (15-ounce) can black beans, rinsed and drained

½ cup chopped fresh basil

½ cup chopped Italian parsley

1 avocado, diced

Kernels from 1 ear of cooked corn

Salt and freshly ground black pepper to taste

Toasted baguette rounds

In a large skillet heat olive oil over medium-high heat. Add shrimp and stir continuously until it starts to turn pink, about 1 minute. Add garlic, reduce heat to low, and cook an additional minute. Transfer shrimp to a large bowl. Add the peppers, onions, black beans, basil, parsley, avocado, corn, salt, and pepper and mix well. Spoon the mixture onto toasted baguette rounds.

Note: The bruschetta topping can be prepared up to 6 hours ahead of time. Refrigerate until 1 hour before serving.

8 servings

MIXED GREENS WITH CRISPY TORTILLAS
AND JALAPEÑO VINAIGRETTE

½ cup vegetable oil, for frying tortilla strips

8 corn tortillas, cut into 1-inch strips

10 ounces mixed field greens

2 cups grape tomatoes, halved

1 cup crumbled feta cheese

To prepare the crispy tortillas: In a large skillet heat oil over medium-high heat. Add tortilla strips and fry until golden brown. Drain on paper towels.

To prepare the salad: In a large bowl place field greens, grape tomatoes, and feta cheese. Drizzle Jalapeño Vinaigrette and toss well. Sprinkle with crispy tortilla strips.

Jalapeño Vinaigrette:

1 pound tomatillos, husked

4 jalapeños, roasted

1 bunch fresh cilantro, chopped

4 garlic cloves

1 tablespoon rice vinegar

1 lime, juiced

1 teaspoon salt

1 cup extra-virgin olive oil

To prepare the vinaigrette: In a medium saucepan of simmering water, blanch tomatillos for 5 minutes. Drain and cool slightly. In the bowl of a food processor add the tomatillos, jalepenos, cilantro, garlic, rice vinegar, lime juice, and salt. With the motor running, slowly drizzle the olive oil and mix until smooth.

Note: *The Crispy Tortillas can be prepared up to 24 hours in advance and stored in an airtight container.*

8 servings

MESQUITE GRILLED STEAK WITH CHIMICHURRI SAUCE

½ cup extra-virgin olive oil
4 garlic cloves, minced
1 teaspoon salt
1 teaspoon freshly ground pepper
2½ pounds tri-tip steaks
3 cups mesquite wood smoke chips
1 (8-inch) square disposable aluminum foil baking pan
Chimichurri Sauce (recipe on page 190)

In a small bowl whisk together the olive oil, garlic, salt, and pepper.

Place steaks in a zip-top bag. Pour marinade over the steaks and marinate in the refrigerator for 2 hours. Remove steaks from refrigerator and bring to room temperature, about thirty minutes before grilling.

Meanwhile, in a large bowl soak wood chips in water for at least 30 minutes.

Heat grill to medium-high heat. Place soaked wood chips in foil pan. Place foil pan directly on top of heat element in bottom of grill. When chips begin to smoke, place steaks on grill directly over chips and cook to desired doneness, about 5 minutes per side for medium-rare. Remove steaks from grill; let stand 5 minutes.

To serve: Thinly slice steaks across the grain. Serve with Chimichurri Sauce drizzled over the top.

8 servings

Chimichurri Sauce:

6 garlic cloves, smashed

1 cup chopped Italian parsley

1 cup fresh cilantro

¼ cup fresh oregano

2 jalapeño peppers, seeds and veins removed

1 tablespoon lime juice

1 teaspoon salt

1 teaspoon freshly ground pepper

¾ cup extra-virgin olive oil

In the bowl of a food processor place garlic, parsley, cilantro, oregano, peppers, lime juice, salt, and pepper. With the motor running, slowly drizzle in the olive oil and blend until smooth. Set aside.

SOUTHWESTERN POTATO SALAD

2 pounds small red-skinned potatoes
Kernels from 1 ear cooked corn
½ cup chopped Vidalia onion
1 (14-ounce) can hearts of palm, drained, cut into ⅓-inch-thick rounds
1¼ cups chopped grape tomatoes
1 poblano pepper, roasted, seeded, peeled, and chopped
½ cup chopped fresh cilantro
Salt
1 avocado, peeled and chopped

In a large pot of boiling salted water cook the potatoes until tender, about 20 minutes. Drain and cool. Cut the potatoes into ½-inch cubes. Place potatoes in a large bowl. Add the corn, onion, hearts of palm, tomatoes, poblano pepper, and cilantro. Drizzle dressing over the potato mixture and toss to coat. Season generously with salt. Gently stir in avocado and serve.

Dressing:
½ cup buttermilk
¼ cup mayonnaise
1 tablespoon fresh lime juice
1½ tablespoons ground cumin
2 teaspoons ground coriander
¼ teaspoon cayenne pepper

In a medium bowl whisk the buttermilk, mayonnaise, lime juice, cumin, coriander, and cayenne until well blended.

8 servings

BLUEBERRY PIE À LA MODE

Filling:

  6 cups blueberries

  1 teaspoon grated lemon zest

  2 tablespoons fresh lemon juice

  6 tablespoons all-purpose flour

  ½ teaspoon ground cinnamon

  ⅛ teaspoon freshly grated nutmeg

  ¾ cup sugar

Crust:

  2 cups all-purpose flour

  ¼ teaspoon salt

  ¾ cup cold unsalted butter, diced

  5 tablespoons cold milk

     Extra flour as needed for rolling

  ½ gallon vanilla ice cream

For the filling: In a large bowl place the blueberries, lemon zest, lemon juice, flour, cinnamon, nutmeg, and sugar. Toss gently until the berries are evenly coated.

For the crust: Heat the oven to 375 degrees. In the bowl of a food processor fitted with a steel blade place the flour and salt. Sprinkle the pieces of butter on top of the flour. Pulse the flour and butter until they are combined and the mixture resembles a coarse meal. Add the milk a tablespoon at a time, pulsing after each addition, until the dough sticks to itself when gently squeezed.

Transfer the dough to a lightly floured surface. Use your hands to shape it into two balls, one twice as large as the other. Using extra flour as needed to prevent sticking, roll the larger ball to fit a 9- or 10-inch pie pan. Line the pie pan with the rolled pie crust and crimp the edges. Pour the filling into the crust.

Roll out the remaining ball of dough. Using a star cookie cutter (any size will do), cut shapes out of the dough and place on top of the filling, overlapping as you go.

Bake 45 minutes or until the filling is bubbling around the edges and the crust is lightly browned. Serve with a scoop of vanilla ice cream.

8 servings

Shopping List

Produce

- 1 small onion
- 1 garlic bulb
- 4 ears corn
- 1 jalepeño pepper
- 1 pint grape tomatoes
- 1 bunch fresh basil
- 1 small red onion
- 1 lemon
- 6 ounces arugula
- 3 ounces mixed baby greens
- 8 strawberries
- 5½ pounds sweet potatoes
- 1 bunch green onions
- 1½ pounds green beans

Meat and dairy

- ¼ pound bacon
- 2 cups finely cooked chicken
- 1 (10-ounce) goat cheese log
- 2 large eggs
- 3 tablespoons unsalted butter
- 2 tablespoons half-and-half

Seafood

- 8 (6-ounce) salmon fillets

Frozen foods

- 1 pint raspberry sorbet
- 1 pint lemon sorbet
- 1 pint mango sorbet
- 1 pint Edy's slow-churned vanilla ice cream
- 1 (10-ounce) package frozen lima beans
- 1 (10-ounce) package frozen raspberries

Other groceries

- Cider vinegar
- 1 package won ton wrappers
- Sugar
- Red wine vinegar
- Dry mustard
- Salt
- Pepper
- Extra-virgin olive oil
- Cooking spray
- Poppy seeds
- All-purpose flour
- Almonds
- Smoked Spanish paprika
- Brown sugar
- New Mexico red chile powder
- Chipolte chile powder
- Ground cumin
- Ground coriander
- Pure maple syrup
- 2 cedar planks
- 1 can chipotle chile peppers in adobo sauce
- 1½ tablespoons miso paste
- Soy sauce
- Rice vinegar
- 1 teaspoon sesame seeds
- Peanut oil
- Chile-garlic sauce
- Cornstarch
- Sesame oil
- 10 shortbread cookies
- 1 jar Bonne Maman wild blueberry preserves

Wine and spirits

- 2 tablespoons sake

Plan Ahead

1 month ahead:
Make and freeze won ton shells

5 days ahead:
Make terrine and freeze

2 days ahead:
Make rub for salmon
Make salad dressing

1 day ahead:
Make filling for won tons
Wash and trim green beans
Make sweet potatoes to the step just before baking and refrigerate

8 hours ahead:
Prepare goat cheese to point just before baking

6 hours ahead:
Put rub on salmon and refrigerate

3 hours ahead:
Slice strawberries for salad

1 hour ahead:
Soak cedar plank

Chicken and Succotash Salad Served in Crisp Won Ton Shells

Strawberry and Arugula Salad with Almond Crusted Goat Cheese Medallions

Whipped Chipotle Sweet Potatoes

Chile Rubbed Salmon Grilled on Cedar Planks

Sesame Spiked Green Beans

Vanilla Ice Cream, Shortbread Cookies,
and Mixed Berry Sorbet Terrine

I love the balance of sweet and spicy flavors throughout this menu. If you haven't tried grilling on cedar planks with its smoky infusion, get ready—you will be hooked. Once you close the lid of the grill you just sit back and wait until it's time to brush on the glaze. There's no flipping involved. The sesame green beans add color and contrast to the chipotle sweet potatoes. The flavors are spectacular together. You will cool off with this "make ahead" frozen dessert. I love cookies and ice cream, so this is one of my favorites.

WINE PAIRING: A Pinot Noir will stand up to the rich flavor of the grilled salmon.

EQUIPMENT: food processor, mini-muffin tin, 2 cedar planks

Tip: You may purchase cedar planks from your local grocery store (sometimes a seasonal item), from hardware stores, cooking stores, or online. Be sure to soak them in water for at least an hour before grilling to prevent scorching.

CHICKEN AND SUCCOTASH SALAD
IN CRISP WON TON SHELLS

Won Ton Shells:
- 1 package won ton wrappers
- Cooking spray

For the won ton shells: Preheat the oven to 350 degrees. Trim the won ton wrappers to form 2-inch squares. Coat a nonstick mini-muffin tin with cooking spray and press a won ton square into each cup. Lightly coat the squares with cooking spray and bake for about 7 minutes or until lightly browned. Repeat the process with the remaining wrappers.

Note: The won tons may be prepared up to 1 week ahead of time if stored in an airtight container in a cabinet or up to 1 month ahead if placed in freezer bags and stored in the freezer.

Chicken and Succotash Salad:
- ¼ pound bacon, chopped
- 1 small onion, chopped
- 2 garlic cloves, minced
- 4 ears corn, kernels cut off and cobs discarded
- 1 jalapeño chile, seeded and finely chopped
- 1 (10-ounce) package frozen baby lima beans, thawed
- 1 pint grape tomatoes, halved
- 2 tablespoons cider vinegar
- 2 cups finely chopped cooked chicken
- ½ cup chopped fresh basil
- Salt and freshly ground pepper, to taste

For the salad: In a large skillet cook the bacon over medium heat until crisp. Drain on paper towels. Reserve 1 tablespoon of the bacon drippings in the skillet.

Add the onion to the skillet and cook over medium heat, stirring until softened. Add garlic and cook an additional 30 seconds. Stir in the corn, jalapeño, lima beans, and tomatoes. Cook, stirring, until the vegetables are tender, about 5 minutes. Stir in vinegar, mixing well.

Transfer the mixture to a large bowl and allow to cool. Add the chicken, bacon, basil, salt, and pepper. Mix well.

To assemble: Fill won ton cups. Serve immediately.

Note: *The filling may be made a day in advance. Cover and refrigerate. Bring to room temperature before filling won ton cups.*

8 servings

STRAWBERRY AND ARUGULA SALAD
WITH ALMOND CRUSTED GOAT CHEESE MEDALLIONS

⅓ cup all-purpose flour

2 large eggs

2 tablespoons water

1 cup sliced almonds

1 (10-ounce) goat cheese log, cut into 8 round slices

6 ounces arugula

3 ounces mixed baby greens

8 strawberries, trimmed and sliced

4 tablespoons extra-virgin olive oil

   Raspberry Vinaigrette (recipe on page 200)

Preheat the oven to 350 degrees. Place three small bowls on your kitchen counter. In the first bowl place the flour. In the second bowl whisk the eggs and water together. In the third bowl place the almonds. Roll the goat cheese slice in flour, dip it in the egg wash, and roll it in the almonds to coat, pressing gently to adhere. Place cheese round in a square glass baking dish. Repeat with remaining cheese rounds. Bake until the almonds are lightly browned, about 10 minutes.

Combine arugula and mixed greens together in a medium bowl. Divide among plates and top with strawberries. Drizzle the salads with olive oil and vinaigrette. Top with a warm goat cheese medallion. *continued on next page* ◗

8 servings

Raspberry Vinaigrette:

⅔ cup frozen raspberries, thawed

½ cup sugar

¼ cup red wine vinegar

2 tablespoons minced red onion

1 tablespoon dry mustard

½ teaspoon salt

½ teaspoon lemon juice

1 cup extra-virgin olive oil

1 tablespoon poppy seeds

In a food processor combine the raspberries, sugar, vinegar, onion, dry mustard, salt, and lemon juice and blend. With motor running, gradually add oil until mixture is smooth. Add poppy seeds and blend 5 seconds.

WHIPPED CHIPOTLE SWEET POTATOES

5½ pounds sweet potatoes, scrubbed
½ tablespoon minced chipotle chiles in adobo
3 tablespoons unsalted butter, cut into pieces and softened
2 tablespoons half-and-half
1 teaspoon salt
½ teaspoon pepper

Put oven rack in middle position and preheat the oven to 450 degrees. Line a baking sheet with foil. Prick each potato several times with a fork. Place on baking sheet and bake until very soft, 1 to 1½ hours.

Reduce the oven temperature to 350 degrees. Butter a glass or ceramic baking dish. When cool enough to handle, halve the potatoes and scoop the flesh into a large bowl. With an electric mixer beat the potatoes, chipotle chiles, butter, half-and-half, salt, and pepper until smooth. Spread potatoes in the buttered baking dish. Bake until hot, 20 to 25 minutes.

8 to 10 servings

CHILE RUBBED SALMON GRILLED ON CEDAR PLANKS

2 teaspoons smoked Spanish paprika

½ teaspoon firmly packed brown sugar

2 teaspoons New Mexico red chile powder

½ teaspoon chipotle chile powder

1 teaspoon ground cumin

½ teaspoon ground coriander

1 teaspoon kosher salt

8 (6-ounce) salmon fillets

2 cedar planks

2 tablespoons pure maple syrup

In a small bowl combine the paprika, brown sugar, chile powders, cumin, coriander, and salt. Rub spice mixture onto both sides of the salmon and place in a covered dish. Marinate in the refrigerator 2 to 6 hours before grilling.

Meanwhile, soak cedar planks submerged in water for 30 minutes. Preheat grill to medium. Place cedar planks on grill surface. Place salmon fillets on the cedar plank. Close the lid on the grill and cook salmon about 30 minutes. Drizzle maple syrup over the salmon fillets and remove cedar plank with salmon from grill. Serve over a bed of Whipped Chipotle Sweet Potatoes.

8 servings

SESAME SPIKED GREEN BEANS

¾ cup water

3 tablespoons sugar

2 tablespoons sake

1½ tablespoons miso

1 tablespoon soy sauce

1 tablespoon rice vinegar

1 tablespoon cornstarch

1½ tablespoons chile-garlic sauce

3 tablespoons peanut oil

1½ pounds green beans, cut into 2-inch lengths

3 green onions, thickly sliced

1 teaspoon sesame oil

1 teaspoon sesame seeds

In a medium bowl, combine the water, sugar, sake, miso, soy sauce, vinegar, cornstarch, and chile-garlic sauce.

Heat a wok or large deep skillet for 2 minutes. Add the oil and heat until almost smoking. Add the green beans and green onions and cook over high heat, stirring occasionally, until just tender and browned in spots, about 6 minutes. Stir in the sauce mixture and bring to a boil. Cook until the sauce is glossy and slightly thickened, about 1 minute. Stir in the sesame oil. Transfer the beans to a platter and garnish with the sesame seeds.

8 servings

VANILLA ICE CREAM, SHORTBREAD COOKIES, AND MIXED BERRY SORBET TERRINE

10 shortbread cookies
1 pint raspberry sorbet
1 pint mango sorbet
1 pint Edy's slow-churned vanilla bean ice cream (or your favorite brand)
1 pint lemon sorbet
1 jar Bonne Maman wild blueberry preserves

For the terrine: Line a 9 x 5 x 2¾-inch metal loaf pan with several layers of plastic wrap, extending 3 inches over the sides. Place cookies in a food processor and pulse into coarse crumbs. Put crumbs in the bottom of the loaf pan. In a medium bowl place the raspberry sorbet and stir to soften. Let stand at room temperature until sorbet is spreadable, stirring occasionally, about 10 minutes. Spread sorbet evenly in bottom of prepared loaf pan. Place the loaf pan in the freezer.

Repeat the same procedure with the mango sorbet, vanilla ice cream, and the lemon sorbet, spooning each layer on top of the last and freezing until the next layer is ready.

Fold plastic wrap overhang over the pan and cover with aluminum foil. Freeze overnight, or up to five days. Invert terrine onto cutting board. Cut it into slices. Warm a jar of wild blueberry preserves in the microwave for 1 minute. Drizzle wild blueberry sauce over terrine slices and serve.

Note: The terrine can be made up to 5 days ahead. Keep frozen.

10 servings

Shopping List

Produce

1 bunch fresh thyme leaves
1 large sweet onion, such as Vidalia
2 red peppers
1 yellow pepper
1 bunch fresh rosemary
1 bunch fresh basil
1 bunch fresh Italian parsley
1 garlic bulb
4 plum tomatoes
1 pound asparagus
1 shallot
6 ounces baby spinach
2 cups baby arugula
4 large limes
2 bunches fresh cilantro
1 orange
1 jalapeño pepper
1 pint raspberries
1 bunch fresh mint leaves

Dairy

2 cups unsalted butter
1 cup grated mozzarella cheese
4 ounces goat cheese
2 cups heavy whipping cream

Seafood

8 (6-ounce) portions swordfish
   steaks

Other groceries

All-purpose flour
Salt
Freshly ground pepper
Dijon mustard
Extra-virgin olive oil
1 can artichoke hearts
Red wine vinegar
Ground cumin
Cajun seasoning
1½ cups jasmine rice
3 cups chicken broth
10 ounces Ghirardelli dark chocolate
   chips
8 small balloons
2 (10-ounce) boxes frozen
   raspberries in syrup
2 teaspoons unflavored gelatin
Powdered sugar

Wine and spirits

2 tablespoons raspberry-flavored
   liqueur

Plan Ahead

2 months ahead:
Make southwestern butter and freeze

1 month ahead:
Make tartlet shells and freeze

5 days ahead:
Make chocolate bowls for dessert

1 day ahead:
Make salad dressing
Make marinade for fish
Make mousse for dessert

8 hours ahead:
Make filling for tartlets
Bake tartlets and keep at room
temperature until ready to reheat
Sauté vegetables for salad

2 hours ahead:
Make rice and keep warm in a heavy
gauge saucepan

Artichoke and Tomato Tartlets

Spinach Salad with Sautéed Asparagus,
Red Peppers, Shallots, and Goat Cheese

Grilled Swordfish with Southwestern Butter

Confetti Rice

Chocolate Cups Filled with Raspberry Mousse

Your garden tomatoes and fresh herbs take the spotlight in these little tartlets. The mozzarella melts into the crust and blends beautifully with the caramelized onions and peppers—yum! If you have children at home, they will love to help dip the balloons in melted chocolate to make the dessert cups.

WINE PAIRING: A chilled bottle of Chardonnay will accentuate the buttery flavors of the tartlets and swordfish.

EQUIPMENT: food processor, 32 (2½ to 3½-inch) fluted edge tartlet pans, 8 small balloons

Tip: Compound butter (such as the Southwestern butter in this menu) can be made with a variety of ingredients. Experiment with different herbs, citrus zest, and even blue cheese. When made ahead and frozen, you can quickly slice some of the butter and let it melt into your grilled chicken, fish, or steak. What a great way to add flavor!

ARTICHOKE AND TOMATO TARTLETS

Crust:

1¼ cups all-purpose flour

1 tablespoon fresh thyme leaves

½ teaspoon salt

   Freshly ground pepper to taste

8 tablespoons (1 stick) cold unsalted butter, cut into small pieces

2 teaspoons Dijon mustard

4 tablespoons ice water

For the crust: In the bowl of a food processor combine the flour, thyme, salt, and pepper. Add the butter and pulse until mixture resembles coarse meal. Add the mustard and enough ice water for the mixture to hold together. Form the dough into one thin disc. Wrap in plastic wrap and chill in the refrigerator for at least one hour.

Filling:

4 tablespoons extra-virgin olive oil

½ large sweet onion, thinly sliced

1 red bell pepper, seeded and thinly sliced

1 yellow bell pepper, seeded and thinly sliced

1 tablespoon fresh thyme

1 tablespoon chopped fresh rosemary

   Salt and freshly ground pepper to taste

3 artichoke hearts (canned), finely chopped

⅓ cup fresh basil, thinly sliced

¼ cup chopped Italian flat leaf parsley

4 garlic cloves, minced

continued on next page ❍

For the filling: Heat the oil in a large, heavy pot over medium-low heat. Add the onions, peppers, thyme, rosemary, and salt and pepper. Cook uncovered, stirring frequently until the vegetables are soft and the mixture resembles marmalade, about 45 minutes. Add the artichoke hearts, basil, parsley, and garlic and cook an additional 5 minutes, stirring frequently. Drain the vegetables well and reserve.

Topping:

  1 cup grated mozzarella cheese

  4 plum tomatoes, cut into ¼-inch slices

  ¼ teaspoon freshly ground pepper

  2 tablespoons fresh thyme

  1 tablespoon chopped Italian parsley

  1 tablespoon extra-virgin olive oil

For the assembly: Preheat the oven to 375 degrees. On a lightly floured surface, roll out the dough to ⅛-inch thickness. Stamp out tartlet shapes and press dough into pans. Using a fork, prick the bottom of each crust. Re-roll the dough and continue this process until all of the dough is used. Place tartlet pans on a baking sheet and bake 10 minutes. Allow tartlets to cool and remove from pans. Spread the mozzarella cheese over the bottom of the tartlet shells. Spread the filling over the cheese. Top with tomatoes. Sprinkle with the pepper, thyme, and basil and drizzle with olive oil and bake for 10 minutes.

Note: Prepare tartlet crusts up to 1 month in advance and freeze.

Makes 32 tartlets

SPINACH SALAD WITH SAUTÉED ASPARAGUS, RED PEPPERS, SHALLOTS, AND GOAT CHEESE

- 6 tablespoons extra-virgin olive oil, divided
- 1 red bell pepper, cut into 1 x 4-inch strips
- 1 pound asparagus, trimmed and cut on diagonal into 1-inch pieces
- ½ teaspoon salt, divided
- ¼ teaspoon freshly ground pepper, divided
- 1 medium shallot, thinly sliced (about ¼ cup)

- 1 tablespoon plus 1 teaspoon red wine vinegar
- 1 medium garlic clove, minced
- ½ cup basil leaves
- 1 bag (6 ounces) baby spinach
- 2 cups baby arugula
- 4 ounces goat cheese, cut into small chunks

In a 12-inch nonstick skillet heat 2 tablespoons oil over high heat until beginning to smoke. Add red pepper and cook until lightly browned, about 2 minutes, stirring once after 1 minute. Add asparagus, ¼ teaspoon salt, and ⅛ teaspoon pepper. Cook until asparagus is browned and almost tender, about 2 minutes, stirring once after 1 minute. Stir in shallot and cook until softened and asparagus is tender-crisp, about one minute. Transfer to a large plate and cool 5 minutes.

Meanwhile, in medium bowl whisk the remaining 4 tablespoons oil, vinegar, garlic, ¼ teaspoon salt, ⅛ teaspoon pepper until combined.

Stack the basil leaves on top of one another. Starting from the top of the leaf, roll up tightly. Using a sharp knife cut the roll into strips to make a chiffonade.

In a large bowl, toss the spinach, basil, and arugula with the dressing and divide among salad plates. Sprinkle with goat cheese.

8 servings

GRILLED SWORDFISH WITH SOUTHWESTERN BUTTER

⅓ cup freshly squeezed lime juice
⅔ cup extra-virgin olive oil
2 garlic cloves, minced
1 teaspoon ground cumin
1 teaspoon Cajun seasoning
½ cup chopped fresh cilantro
8 (6-ounce) portions swordfish steaks
Southwestern Butter (recipe on page 213)

In a medium bowl combine the lime juice, olive oil, garlic, cumin, Cajun seasoning, and cilantro. Place swordfish steaks in a 9 x 13-inch glass baking dish. Pour marinade over fish. Cover the dish with plastic wrap and refrigerate 30 minutes, turning the fish halfway through.

Preheat grill to medium-high. Grill the fish approximately 4 minutes per side. Turn heat off and top each swordfish steak with 1½ tablespoons Southwestern Butter. Close the lid and allow the butter to melt onto the fish, about 1 minute. Remove swordfish from the grill and serve.

8 servings

Southwestern Butter:

½ cup unsalted butter, softened

1½ teaspoons Cajun seasoning

¾ teaspoon ground cumin

½ cup chopped fresh cilantro

1 garlic clove, minced

In the bowl of a food processor combine the butter, Cajun seasoning, cumin, cilantro, and garlic. Pulse until combined well. Transfer butter to a sheet of plastic wrap, shaping into a log. Cover with sides of plastic wrap and roll up to close. Refrigerate 2 hours to set. Slice into 1½-tablespoon segments for melting.

Note: The Southwestern Butter may be made up to 1 week in advance if stored in the refrigerator, or up to 2 months in advance if frozen.

CONFETTI RICE

 2 tablespoons extra-virgin olive oil
 ½ cup chopped Vidalia onion
 1 jalapeño pepper, seeded and minced
 1½ cups jasmine rice
 3 cups chicken broth
 2 teaspoons minced orange zest
 ½ cup chopped fresh cilantro
   Salt and pepper to taste

In a medium saucepan over medium-high heat, add oil and sauté onion and jalapeño until softened, about 4 minutes. Add the rice and continue to sauté until rice is golden, about 2 additional minutes. Add the chicken broth and orange zest and bring to a boil. Reduce heat to low and cook 2 minutes. Remove from heat and toss with cilantro. Season with salt and pepper.

8 servings

My husband and I really enjoy cooking and entertaining, so we decided to make this menu in its entirety for our supper club. We followed Debi's plan to make things ahead and it really paid off! It was nice not having to think about what needed to be done; we just got to work and checked things off as we went.

The Tomato Tartlets were out of this world! We were able to use the last of the summer tomatoes from the farmers' market. The swordfish was very easy to make and would be a great weeknight entrée. We had some Southwestern Butter left over, which we will keep in the freezer for the next time.

Yum!

GARRET AND MOLLY

CHOCOLATE CUPS FILLED WITH RASPBERRY MOUSSE

Chocolate Cups:

8 small balloons

10 ounces Ghirardelli dark chocolate chips

Set aside a baking sheet lined with parchment paper.

Blow up 8 balloons (about 4 to 5 inches in diameter when fully inflated).

In a medium microwave-safe bowl add the chocolate and microwave in 25-second intervals until melted. Stir until smooth.

Spoon 1 teaspoon melted chocolate onto prepared pan to form a small disk. Dip a balloon into the bowl of melted chocolate, coating about one-third of the balloon.

Place dipped end on chocolate disk. Repeat with remaining balloons and chocolate. Transfer the pan to the refrigerator to set, about 30 minutes.

To release air from the balloons, pinch each balloon just under the knot, and cut a small hole in the surface between your fingers and the knot. Very gradually release the air; if air is released too quickly, the cups may break. Carefully peel the deflated balloons from the chocolate cups, and patch any holes with the remaining chocolate. Return the chocolate cups to the refrigerator until ready to use.

Raspberry Mousse:

 2 (10-ounce) boxes frozen raspberries in syrup, thawed
 2 tablespoons raspberry liqueur
 2 teaspoons unflavored gelatin
 2 cups chilled heavy whipping cream
 ½ cup powdered sugar

Garnish:

  Fresh raspberries
  Mint sprigs
 ¼ cup powdered sugar

In a food processor purée thawed raspberries. Over a heavy, small saucepan strain raspberries through a coarse sieve, pressing on seeds with the back of a spoon. Over medium heat cook raspberry purée until reduced to 1 cup, stirring occasionally, about 15 minutes.

Meanwhile, in a small bowl place the raspberry liqueur. Sprinkle the gelatin over the liqueur and let mixture stand 10 minutes to soften.

Add gelatin mixture to hot raspberry purée and stir to dissolve the gelatin. Pour puree into a large bowl. Cool completely, stirring occasionally.

In a medium bowl whip the cream and powdered sugar to stiff peaks. Fold the whipped cream into purée in 2 additions. Refrigerate 2 to 4hours.

continued on next page ○

Fill a pastry bag fitted with a star decorating tip with mousse. Pipe mousse into cup three-fourths of the way up.

To serve: Garnish with fresh raspberries and mint sprigs. Dust with powdered sugar.

Note: *You can make the chocolate cups up to 5 days ahead. Refrigerate until ready to use.*

8 servings

Shopping List

Produce

1 stem fresh lemon grass
1 (2-inch) piece ginger
1 garlic bulb
1 bunch green onions
1 red bell pepper
1 lime
1 bunch fresh thyme leaves
2 red beets
4 medium fennel bulbs
1 cup micro greens
4 zucchini
1 lemon
2 large shallots
1 bunch fresh basil
3 Roma tomatoes
1 pint fresh raspberries

Dairy

½ cup milk
¾ cup unsalted butter
2 large eggs
½ cup sour cream
2 cups heavy whipping cream
2 tablespoons unsalted butter

Seafood

32 large shrimp
8 (6-ounce) halibut steaks

Other groceries

Soy sauce
Sesame oil
Dried red pepper flakes
Honey
Peanut oil
Bamboo skewers
White balsamic vinegar
Extra-virgin olive oil
1½ cups packaged sugared walnuts (such as Emerald brand)
1 (14-ounce) can coconut milk
3½ ounces panko bread crumbs
Canola oil
Salt
Pepper
Cake flour
Baking soda
1⅛ cups firmly packed light brown sugar
2 ounces unsweetened chocolate
Vanilla extract
Coffee
1 (10-ounce) box frozen raspberries in syrup
Unflavored gelatin
Powdered sugar
Sugar
12 ounces semisweet chocolate chips

Wine and spirits

1 cup white wine
1 tablespoon raspberry liqueur

Plan Ahead

1 week ahead:
Bake cake and freeze

2 days ahead:
Make mousse

1 day ahead:
Make marinade for shrimp
Pulse panko crumbs in the food processor
Roast beets
Make salad dressing
Assemble cake

2 hours ahead:
Make sauce for fish
Peel zucchini

Lemon Grass and Ginger Shrimp Kebabs

Roasted Beet, Fennel, and Sugared Walnut Salad

Crispy Halibut with Lemony Basil Sauce

Chocolate Raspberry Mousse Cake

In the warm months of summer, we often find ourselves at the beach looking for that ocean breeze. My friends Susan and Charlie created a really fun tablescape that would work well with this menu. The table was decorated with a sea-blue cloth, fishing net, shells, and low-lit candles. An under-the-sea DVD on a movie screen beside the dinner table added to the ambiance, and we felt as if we were next to a live aquarium! This menu is light and refreshing with hints of lemon, fennel, and basil. The zucchini ribbons add movement to the plate with their delicate curves. Fresh summer raspberries adorn the Chocolate Raspberry Mousse Cake—the most requested recipe at my wedding cake business in San Francisco.

WINE PAIRING: A crisp Sauvignon Blanc with its acidity will balance the lemon in the cream sauce.

EQUIPMENT: bamboo skewers

Tip: Freezing a cake before decorating creates a much more stable cake and eliminates the crumbs into the icing problem that everyone dreads.

LEMON GRASS AND GINGER SHRIMP KEBABS

1 tablespoon chopped lemon grass

1 tablespoon chopped fresh ginger

2 garlic cloves, minced

½ teaspoon dried red pepper flakes

5 green onions, whites cut into 1½-inch lengths
and greens chopped

¼ cup soy sauce

2 tablespoons sesame oil

1 tablespoon honey

32 large shrimp, shelled and deveined
Bamboo skewers soaked in water for at least 30 minutes

1 red bell pepper, seeded and cut into 1½-inch pieces
Peanut oil for drizzling

1 lime, juiced

In a large bowl, combine the lemon grass, ginger, garlic, red pepper flakes, chopped green onions, soy sauce, sesame oil, and honey. Whisk well. Add the shrimp and toss to coat. Marinate in the refrigerator for 15 to 30 minutes.

Meanwhile, soak the skewers in water for at least 30 minutes.

Skewer the shrimp, white portion of green onion, and red bell peppers. Place the skewers on a large baking sheet and drizzle with peanut oil. Grill skewers over high heat about 3 minutes per side (until shrimp curl and begin to pink). Remove skewers from the grill and squeeze a bit of lime juice over each skewer before serving.

8 servings

ROASTED BEET, FENNEL, AND SUGARED WALNUT SALAD

Salad:
- 2 red beets, trimmed and scrubbed clean
- ¼ cup extra-virgin olive oil
- Salt and freshly ground pepper
- 4 medium fennel bulbs, trimmed and thinly sliced
- 1½ cups packaged sugared walnuts (such as Emerald brand)
- 1 cup micro greens

Dressing:
- ¼ cup white balsamic vinegar
- 2 tablespoons minced shallots
- 2 teaspoons sugar
- 1 teaspoon salt
- 1 teaspoon freshly ground pepper
- ¼ cup milk
- 2 tablespoons fresh thyme leaves
- 1 cup extra-virgin olive oil

For the salad: Preheat the oven to 350 degrees. In a medium bowl toss the beets with olive oil. Season with salt and pepper and transfer to a baking dish. Cover with foil and bake 55 minutes. Cool beets, peel, and cut into a 1-inch dice.

For the dressing: In a medium bowl whisk the balsamic vinegar, shallots, sugar, salt, pepper, milk, thyme, and olive oil. Chill until ready to dress the salad.

To assemble: Combine the beets, fennel, and sugared walnuts together in a salad bowl. Add the desired amount of dressing and toss well. Adjust seasoning with salt and pepper. Spoon onto plates and garnish with a generous pinch of micro greens in the center of each salad.

8 servings

CRISPY HALIBUT WITH LEMONY BASIL SAUCE

Sauce:

½ cup unsalted butter, cut into tablespoons

3 tablespoons minced shallots

1 cup white wine

Juice and zest from 1 lemon

3 Roma tomatoes, diced

½ cup chopped fresh basil

¼ teaspoon salt

¼ teaspoon freshly ground pepper

Zucchini Ribbons:

4 zucchini, ends trimmed

1 (14-ounce) can coconut milk

Halibut:

3½ ounces panko bread crumbs

½ cup milk

8 (6-ounce) halibut steaks (or other firm white-fleshed fish)

Salt and pepper

Canola oil

For the sauce: In a medium saucepan melt 2 tablespoons of the butter over medium heat. Add shallots and cook until shallots soften a bit, about 3 minutes. Add the wine and lemon zest. Increase heat to high and bring to a boil. Reduce by one-third. Reduce heat to medium, add the lemon juice, and begin whisking in the remaining butter, 1 tablespoon at a time to finish the sauce. Remove from heat and add the tomatoes and basil. Adjust seasoning with salt and freshly ground pepper.

For the zucchini ribbons: Using a vegetable peeler, slice the zucchini into very thin pieces. In a large sauté pan bring coconut milk to a boil over medium-high heat. Add the zucchini and cook, stirring, 2 minutes. *continued on next page* ❍

For the fish: In a food processor pulse panko crumbs into a fine powder and transfer to a plate. In a shallow bowl pour the milk. Season the halibut with salt and pepper. Dip each halibut steak in milk, then into the plate of panko crumbs. Press the crumbs onto both sides of fish. Place a large sauté pan over medium-high heat. Add enough canola oil to just cover the bottom of the pan. Heat oil, then add halibut to the pan. (Be careful to not overcrowd the fish. Wipe out the pan and repeat the searing process in batches, if necessary.) Cook until a golden crust begins to form on the bottom of fish, about 6 minutes. Flip and cook on the other side an additional 4 to 5 minutes.

To serve: Using tongs, divide the zucchini among plates. Place fish on top of the zucchini and spoon the sauce over the fish.

8 servings

CHOCOLATE RASPBERRY MOUSSE CAKE

Cake:

- 1 cup cake flour
- 1 teaspoon baking soda
- ¼ teaspoon salt
- ¼ cup unsalted butter, softened
- 1⅛ cups firmly packed light brown sugar
- 2 large eggs
- 2 ounces unsweetened chocolate, melted and cooled
- ¾ teaspoon vanilla extract
- ½ cup sour cream
- ½ cup very strong hot brewed coffee

Grease and flour a 9-inch round pan and line with parchment paper. Set aside.

Sift together the flour, baking soda, and salt. With an electric mixer beat the butter, brown sugar, and eggs for 5 minutes, until very light and fluffy. Beat in cooled chocolate and vanilla.

Stir in about one-third of the dry ingredients, half of the sour cream, another one-third of the dry ingredients, the rest of the sour cream, and finally the remainder of the dry ingredients. Stir until just mixed.

Stir in the hot coffee, pour into the prepared pan, and bake in a preheated 350-degree oven for 35 minutes. Cool pan on a wire rack. Wrap the cake in several layers of plastic wrap and freeze before continuing.   *continued on next page* ❍

Note: The cake can be made up to 2 weeks ahead of time. Freeze until ready to assemble.

Note: The mousse can be made up to 2 days ahead of time. Refrigerate until ready to assemble.

Mousse:

- 1 (10-ounce) box frozen raspberries in syrup, thawed
- 1 tablespoon raspberry liqueur
- 1 teaspoon unflavored gelatin
- 1 cup chilled heavy whipping cream
- ¼ cup powdered sugar

In a food processor purée thawed raspberries. Over a small saucepan strain the raspberries through a coarse sieve, pressing on seeds with the back of a spoon. Over medium heat cook the raspberry purée until reduced to ½ cup, stirring occasionally, about 10 minutes.

Meanwhile, place the raspberry liqueur in a small bowl. Sprinkle the gelatin over the liqueur and let mixture stand 10 minutes to soften. Add the gelatin mixture to hot raspberry purée and stir to dissolve the gelatin. Pour puree into a medium bowl. Cool completely, stirring occasionally. Using an electric mixer, whip cream and powdered sugar until stiff peaks form. Fold the whipped cream into puree in two additions. Refrigerate, covered, until ready to use.

Ganache:
- 1 cup heavy whipping cream
- 2 tablespoons unsalted butter
- 2 tablespoons sugar
- 12 ounces semisweet chocolate chips

In a small saucepan over medium heat, combine the whipping cream, butter, and sugar. Bring the mixture to a simmer. Remove from heat and stir in the chocolate chips, mixing until smooth. Cool ganache to room temperature before applying to the cake.

Garnish:
- 1 pint fresh raspberries

To assemble: Remove cake from the freezer and unwrap. Using a serrated knife, split the cake in half horizontally. Spread an even layer of raspberry mousse on the bottom layer of the cake. Replace top half of cake, cut-side down, over the mousse. On the top of the cake pour a small amount of ganache in the center of cake, spreading with a spatula to distribute to the sides of cake. Continue pouring and spreading ganache until the cake is covered.

Chill uncovered in the refrigerator until set (about 1 hour).

To serve: Arrange fresh raspberries along the outer edge of cake.

8 servings

Shopping List:

Produce

3 large heirloom tomatoes

2 cloves garlic

Fresh basil leaves

3 lemons

5 garlic cloves

Italian parsley

Fresh thyme leaves

Fresh rosemary

1 shallot

Mint leaves

1 small onion

4 ears corn

1 large eggplant

1 zucchini

2 yellow crookneck squash

3 portabello mushrooms

2 red bell peppers

6 large peaches

2 pints blueberries

2 pints raspberries

Bakery

1 baguette

Meat and dairy

6 ounces goat cheese

1 (5-pound) chicken

Shopping Tip: If you don't like cutting up chicken, or you simply don't have the time, look for a pre-cut chicken in the meat department.

Frozen

2 pints vanilla ice cream

Other groceries

Extra-virgin olive oil

Salt

Freshly ground black pepper

Dry mustard

Cayenne pepper

Sherry vinegar

Dijon mustard

1½ cups quinoa

½ cup pine nuts

Balsamic vinegar

1 (14-ounce) can sweetened condensed milk

½ cup (1 stick) unsalted butter

Ground cinnamon

Ground nutmeg

Vanilla extract

All-purpose flour

Kosher salt

Fine cornmeal

Light brown sugar

Old-fashioned rolled oats (not instant)

¾ cup (3 ounces) chopped pecans

Plan ahead

8 hours ahead:

Make quinoa salad

Make marinade for chicken

Wash and prep vegetables, place in a ziplock bag, and refrigerate

4 hours ahead:

Marinate chicken

Make bruschetta topping and let it sit at room temperature

2 hours ahead:

Marinate vegetables

1 hour ahead:

Grill bread for bruschetta

Assemble dessert, cover with foil, and set aside until ready to bake

30 minutes ahead:

Assemble bruschetta

When guests arrive:

Grill chicken

Put dessert in the oven

Bruschetta with Goat Cheese and Heirloom Tomatoes

Herb Marinated Chicken

Quinoa Corn Salad with Mint Vinaigrette and Toasted Pine Puts

Grilled Vegetables

Peach, Blueberry, and Raspberry Crisp with Dulce de Leche Sauce

I t's summertime, and your local farmers' market has some of the most mouthwatering selections you've ever seen. Now's the time to take advantage of all the fresh, local ingredients. Did you know there is actually an official term for eating locally? A localvore only consumes food that is grown, raised, or produced in the surrounding area (no greater than 100 miles). The benefits of eating local food, even for a night, means you'll not only get pesticide- and hormone-free products, but you'll also be eating food that tastes better, has more nutritional value, and helps to support your local economy.

Why not celebrate this idea with a "Going Local" party?

BRUSCHETTA WITH GOAT CHEESE
AND HEIRLOOM TOMATOES

3 large heirloom tomatoes, diced

2 garlic cloves, minced

3 tablespoons extra-virgin olive oil

½ teaspoon salt

½ teaspoon freshly ground pepper

½ cup chopped fresh basil leaves

1 teaspoon grated lemon zest

1 baguette, sliced into 1-inch-thick slices

1 garlic clove, halved

6 ounces goat cheese, softened

In a medium bowl, mix together tomatoes, minced garlic, olive oil, salt, pepper, basil, and lemon zest. Set aside.

Heat grill to medium-high heat. Place baguette slices on grill and lightly toast on each side. Remove baguette slices from grill and rub one side with garlic clove. Spread about 1 teaspoon of softened goat cheese on each baguette slice. Top with a spoonful of tomato mixture.

8 servings

HERB MARINATED CHICKEN

1½ cups extra-virgin olive oil

¾ cup lemon juice

¾ cup chopped Italian parsley

¼ cup fresh thyme leaves

2 tablespoons chopped fresh rosemary

4 cloves garlic, minced

1 tablespoon dry mustard

1½ tablespoons ground black pepper

½ teaspoon cayenne pepper

1 teaspoon salt

1 (5-pound) chicken, cut into serving pieces

In a medium bowl, add the olive oil, lemon juice, parsley, thyme, rosemary, garlic, dry mustard, peppers, and salt. Mix until combined; add chicken and turn to coat. Transfer to a ziplock bag and marinate in the refrigerator 2 to 4 hours.

Heat grill to medium-high. Remove the chicken pieces from the marinade and grill until cooked through. The wings will need about 5 minutes per side; the legs, 8 minutes per side; the breasts, 10 minutes per side; and the thighs, 12 minutes per side. Season the chicken with salt and pepper and serve.

8 servings

QUINOA CORN SALAD WITH MINT VINAIGRETTE AND TOASTED PINE NUTS

Quinoa:

½ cup pine nuts
1 tablespoon extra-virgin olive oil
1 small onion, finely chopped
  Pinch of salt
1½ cups quinoa, rinsed
1¼ cups water
4 ears corn, kernels removed

Heat oven to 350 degrees. Place pine nuts on a baking sheet and bake until golden brown and fragrant, about 8 minutes. Set aside.

Heat olive oil in a medium saucepan over medium-high heat. Add onions, sprinkle with salt and sauté 3 minutes, stirring frequently. Add quinoa and continue to sauté an additional 2 minutes. Add water and bring to a boil. Cover, reduce heat, and simmer 10 minutes. Add corn kernels to pan, cover, and continue to cook an additional 5 minutes. Transfer quinoa corn mixture to a large bowl and toss with a spoon to loosen. Cool to room temperature. Add dressing and pine nuts. Mix well.

Dressing:

- 2 tablespoons fresh lemon juice
- 2 tablespoons Sherry vinegar
- 1 tablespoon Dijon mustard
- 1 tablespoon minced shallot
- ½ cup chopped mint leaves
- ¾ teaspoon salt
- ½ tablespoon freshly ground pepper
- ½ cup extra-virgin olive oil

In a medium bowl whisk together the lemon juice, Sherry vinegar, Dijon mustard, shallot, mint, salt, pepper, and olive oil and set aside.

8 servings

Shopping Tip: If your grocery store doesn't stock quinoa, ask the store manager if they can order it for you.

GRILLED VEGETABLES

  1 cup extra-virgin olive oil

  1 cup Balsamic vinegar

  1 large eggplant, peeled and cut into ⅓-inch-thick rounds

  1 zucchini, cut lengthwise into thirds

  2 yellow crookneck squash, cut lengthwise into thirds

  3 portabello mushrooms

  2 red bell peppers, halved lengthwise and seeded

1½ teaspoons salt

  2 teaspoons freshly ground pepper

  ½ cup chopped fresh basil

Brush the vegetables with the olive oil and Balsamic vinegar. Heat grill to medium-high. Add vegetables and grill 3 to 5 minutes per side until well browned. Transfer grilled vegetables to a cutting board. Cut into 1-inch-thick pieces and transfer to serving platter. Season with salt and pepper and sprinkle with chopped fresh basil.

8 servings

PEACH, BLUEBERRY, AND RASPBERRY CRISP WITH DULCE DE LECHE SAUCE

1 (14-ounce) can sweetened condensed milk

Butter to prepare pan

6 large peaches, peeled, pitted, and cut into ½-inch cubes

2 pints blueberries

2 pints raspberries

½ teaspoon ground cinnamon

¼ teaspoon nutmeg

2 tablespoons lemon juice

2 teaspoons vanilla

2 tablespoons flour

½ teaspoon kosher salt

1 cup all-purpose flour

1 cup fine cornmeal

¾ cup firmly packed light brown sugar

¾ cup old-fashioned rolled oats (not instant)

¾ cup (3 ounces) chopped pecans

¼ teaspoon kosher salt

½ teaspoon ground cinnamon

½ cup (1 stick) unsalted butter, at room temperature, cut into ½-inch pieces

2 teaspoons vanilla extract

2 pints vanilla ice cream

To make the dulce de leche: Immerse the unopened can of sweetened condensed milk in a pot of water. Bring to a boil and cook for 2 hours, replenishing the water as necessary. Remove from the heat and let cool slightly in the can. Open the can and you will have fresh dulce de leche.

To make the fruit filling: Position rack in the center of the oven and preheat oven to 350 degrees. Butter a large oval gratin pan or 9 x 13-inch baking pan. In a large mixing bowl, combine all the peaches, blueberries, raspberries, dulce de leche, cinnamon, nutmeg, lemon juice, vanilla, flour, and salt. Pour into the prepared pan.

To make the pecan topping: In another bowl, combine the flour, cornmeal, brown sugar, rolled oats, pecans, salt, cinnamon, butter, and vanilla extract and pinch them together with your fingers to make crumbs. Do not overwork the topping. Sprinkle the topping over fruit. *continued on next page* ◯

Bake for 35 to 40 minutes, or until the fruit is tender when pierced with the tip of a sharp knife, the filling is bubbling, and the crumbs are golden brown. Cool on a wire rack for about 20 minutes to let the fruit set.

To serve: Spoon a portion of baked fruit crisp into a bowl and top with a scoop of vanilla ice cream.

12 servings

ACKNOWLEDGMENTS AND THANKS

To everyone at Franklin Green Publishing for making this book possible. You have turned my dream into a reality. Thank you for all you have done to capture my vision and see it through.

To Ron Manville for taking the dishes I prepared and creating such beautiful food art. You made a busy week of shooting a memorable experience.

To Nancy and Chiwon Hahn, dear friends who welcomed us into their home and allowed us to take over their living space with camera gear and lights.

To Carrie Schmidt, my good friend and neighbor for all of your hard work and creativity involved in designing the tablescapes for this book. Thank you for graciously hosting our supper club at your home where we shot the cover for this book and celebrated the photo shoot "wrap".

To all of my "Signature Menus" cooking class students in Richmond. You continue to provide huge support as fans, recipe testers, supper club advisors, and friends. I love you all!

INDEX

TO GET THE MOST OUT OF YOUR DINNER PARTY, PLEASE VISIT

www.debishawcross.com

- Follow Debi's blog

- Download party music playlists

- Try out new recipes

- Learn how to properly set a table

- Discover the best wine pairings for your next dinner party